Greece Travel Guide 2023

Your Comprehensive Tourist guide and information to help you experience Greece like a Pro

Dallas J. Gresham

Copyright

Greece Travel Guide 2023

Your Comprehensive Tourist guide and information to help you experience Greece like a Pro

Your Comprehensive Tourist guide and information to help you

experience Greece like a Pro

INTRODUCTION

For many individuals, visiting Greece may be a once-in-a-lifetime experience. The nation is a well-liked vacation destination for tourists from all over the globe because of its fascinating history, stunning beaches, and delectable food. Yet, without the right advice and knowledge, your vacation to Greece might easily become tedious and perplexing.

Think about landing in Greece without any knowledge of what to do or where to go. You could miss out on some of the greatest activities and experiences the nation has to offer, have trouble finding a place to stay or eat, and feel intimidated by the foreign language and culture. To help you experience Greece like a pro, "Greece Travel Guide 2023: Your Complete Tourist Guide and Information" is available.

This book is intended to help you get the most out of your visit to Greece, stay clear of frequent pitfalls, and take advantage of everything that the nation has to offer. This book will make sure that your vacation to Greece is an unforgettable one by providing in-depth information on the top sights, beaches, and culinary experiences, as well as insider tips and useful recommendations.

This book includes all you need to know to enjoy the finest of Greece, from seeing historic sites and museums to finding undiscovered jewels and quaint towns. In order to assist you in fully immersing yourself in the Greek way of life, it also contains useful information on travel, safety, and cultural etiquette, as well as a section on insider tips from locals.

Thus, pick up "Greece Travel Guide 2023" if you're planning a vacation to Greece and want to escape the aggravation and uncertainty of traveling without a guide. This book will provide you with all the knowledge and ideas you need, whether you're a seasoned traveler or a first-time visitor, to enjoy Greece to the fullest.

With 18 comprehensive chapters covering everything from travel essentials and accommodations to cultural experiences and off-the-beaten-path destinations, this guide is your ultimate companion for exploring Greece.

The "Greece Travel Guide 2023: Your Complete Tourist Guide and Information to Help You Enjoy Greece Like a Pro" website are pleased to welcome you. Greece is a place that has always captivated the hearts and minds of tourists. Greece is a place that has something to offer to everyone with its breathtaking beaches, engrossing history, and distinctive culture.

Whether you're a seasoned traveler or a first-time visitor to Greece, our travel guide will help you get the most out of your trip. It is jam-packed with details on the top sights, experiences, and activities that Greece has to offer, as well as insider knowledge and helpful pointers for navigating the country's distinctive traditions and cultural norms.

This guide includes suggestions for off-the-beaten-path locations that you won't find in other guidebooks as well as thorough information on the finest lodging, food, and transportation alternatives. To make sure you have a pleasant and pleasurable time in Greece, we've also included crucial travel advice, such as safety measures and cultural etiquette.

Yet this manual is more than simply a repository of knowledge and advice. It also honors Greece's illustrious past and culture. Its pages will introduce you to the nation's historical sites, folklore, and mouthwatering cuisine. This book provides something for everyone, whether you're a history buff, a gourmet, or an adventure seeker.

Hence, "Greece Travel Guide 2023" includes everything you need to enjoy Greece like a pro, whether you're planning a romantic visit to the Greek islands, a family holiday in Athens, or a solitary adventure through the countryside. We can't wait to assist you in experiencing the enchantment of this stunning nation and making lifelong memories.

Part I: Before You Go

Chapter 1: Planning Your Trip to Greece

When to Go to Greece

Greece has a Mediterranean climate, which has extended, hot summers and moderate winters. The nation is well-known for its magnificent beaches, beautiful seas, and historic sites, which draw visitors from all over the globe. The date of your visit is one of the most crucial factors to take into account while making travel plans to Greece. The ideal time to visit Greece will be discussed in this Sub chapter, taking into consideration variables like the weather, people, and costs.

The summer months in Greece normally run from June through September, with average highs of 20 to 30 degrees Celsius. Greece is experiencing its busiest travel time right now, with many tourists arriving to take advantage of the islands and beaches. This is the ideal time to go to Greece if you like the beach or participating in water sports. There are plenty of chances to go swimming, sunbathe, and engage in other water sports. You can also attend well-known summer festivals and cultural events.

The drawback to visiting Greece in the peak season is that costs tend to go up and crowds may be oppressive, especially in well-liked tourist hotspots like Santorini and Mykonos. It's also crucial to keep in mind that it may become very hot, especially in August, and that many residents have their own summer vacations around this time, which means certain establishments can be closed.

When planning a trip to Greece, think about going during the shoulder season when prices are lower and the atmosphere is more laid-back. May, early June, and late September to early October are included in this. The weather is still nice, but there are fewer people and the costs are lower. A lot of companies, including restaurants and stores, are still operating.

You may attend cultural events and festivals like the Thessaloniki International Film Festival in November and the Athens Epidaurus Festival in June if you visit Greece during the shoulder season. Also, you may take part in outdoor pursuits like hiking and touring without feeling the effects of the summer heat.

Consider going to Greece in the winter, from November to February, if you're on a limited budget or just want to travel off-peak. Prices are at their lowest during this period, and you may benefit from off-season discounts on lodging and activities. It's vital to keep in mind that many establishments, especially those on the islands, may be closed during this time and that it may be freezing and wet outside.

The ideal time to visit Greece thus depends on your own goals and tastes. Summertime is the greatest time to go on a beach vacation if you don't mind the crowds and higher expenses. Consider vacationing during the shoulder season if you want to avoid large crowds and save money. The winter season is also a fantastic choice if you have a limited travel budget or want to go off-peak. You will undoubtedly be mesmerized by Greece's beauty and culture no matter what time of year you decide to go there.

How to Get to Greece

Greece is a well-liked travel destination in Europe, drawing millions of tourists yearly. Greece may be reached through a variety of modes of transportation, including air, sea, and land. The nation's well-developed transportation infrastructure makes it simple for tourists from throughout the globe to go there. Here we will examine the many options to go to Greece and provide some advice to help you have a comfortable and stress-free trip.

By Air:

The most popular method of travel to Greece is via air, with several international airlines offering nonstop flights to Athens, Thessaloniki, and other significant cities. The primary hub for flights to Greece is Athens International Airport, which is serviced by several carriers, including Aegean Airlines, Olympic Air, and Ryanair. You may go to your destination via taxi, subway, bus, or train from the airport. Thessaloniki, Crete, Rhodes, and Santorini are among the other airports in Greece that are serviced by both local and international airlines.

By Sea:

Greece is renowned for having a large number of islands, thus exploring the nation by water is common. Piraeus and Thessaloniki are the two largest ports in Greece, and many ferries and catamarans link the mainland to the islands. Also, there are international ferries that link Greece to nations like Italy, Turkey, and Cyprus. Anek Lines, Hellenic Seaways, and Blue Star Ferries are a few well-known ferry operators. A trip to Greece is another option if you'd want a more opulent experience since several cruise companies include it on their itineraries.

By Land:

Due to its shared borders with Albania, North Macedonia, Bulgaria, and Turkey, Greece is also accessible via land. Greece is connected to its surrounding nations by a number of bus companies, notably KTEL, and Albtrans. You may enter Greece by car at one of the several land border crossings, but it's crucial to make sure you have all the required paperwork and that your car is roadworthy.

Tips for Traveling to Greece

To guarantee a stress-free vacation, it's crucial to plan your trip in advance regardless of the form of transportation you use. Before visiting Greece, bear the following in mind:

- To obtain the best prices, get your tickets in advance.
- Before flying to Greece, confirm the requirements for your passport and visa.
- Be sure you have all the documentation required for your method of transportation.

- Before visiting Greece, particularly if you're going during the summer, check the weather forecast.
- If you often become seasick when traveling by sea, you may want to think about taking motion sickness medicine.
- Travel light, particularly if you want to visit many islands.
- To help you converse with the locals, learn some fundamental Greek words and phrases.
- Greece may be reached by a number of different routes, making it rather simple for travelers.
- You may travel around this Mediterranean nation's beauty and culture via air, sea, or land.
- You may go to Greece with ease and have a fantastic experience with a little planning and preparation.

Visa and Entry Requirements

Greece is a well-liked vacation spot that draws tourists from all over the globe. Knowing the visa and entrance procedures that apply to your place of origin is crucial if you're considering a trip to Greece.

Depending on your country and the reason for your trip, there are different visa and entrance requirements for Greece. Due to their freedom of movement, tourists from the European Union (EU),

European Economic Area (EEA), and Switzerland often do not need a visa to enter Greece. On the other hand, non-EU nationals must first seek a visa in order to enter the nation.

To enter Greece, you will need a Schengen visa if you are a citizen of a nation that is not a member of the EU or EEA. With a Schengen visa, you may travel to and within the Schengen Area, which is made up of Greece and 25 other European nations. You must submit your application to the Greek embassy or consulate in your country of residence in order to get a Schengen visa. It is crucial to apply well in advance of your intended trip since the application procedure often takes several weeks.

A valid passport or another form of identification, proof of lodging in Greece, evidence of sufficient funds to finance your stay, and a travel itinerary are all requirements for obtaining a Schengen visa. Depending on the reason for your visit, you could also be required to provide a medical certificate, evidence of travel insurance, and other papers. Even if your application is rejected, the visa application cost is non-refundable.

There are additional criteria for admission into Greece in addition to the visa requirements. All travelers must have a current passport that is valid for at least three more months after the date of their intended departure from Greece. You may need to secure extra permissions or documentation if you're going to Greece for a particular reason, like business or school.

Greece is a part of the European Union and the Schengen Area, thus the conditions for admission and visas are subject to change. This is an essential point to keep in mind. To make sure you have the necessary papers and can enter the nation without any problems, it is advised that you verify the most recent criteria before your trip.

It's essential to comprehend the visa and entrance procedures that are relevant to your nation of origin if you're arranging a vacation to Greece. Visitors from the EU, EEA, and Switzerland do not need a visa to enter Greece; however, travelers from other nations must apply for a Schengen visa. Depending on the reason for their trip, all visitors must have a current passport and fulfill extra entrance criteria. To prevent any problems at the border, it's crucial to review the most recent rules before you go.

Health and Safety Considerations

Greece is a well-liked vacation spot that draws tourists from all over the globe. Knowing the visa and entrance procedures that apply to your place of origin is crucial if you're considering a trip to Greece.

Depending on your country and the reason for your trip, there are different visa and entrance requirements for Greece. Due to their freedom of movement, tourists from the European Union (EU), European Economic Area (EEA), and Switzerland often do not need a visa to enter Greece. On the other hand, non-EU nationals must first seek a visa in order to enter the nation.

To enter Greece, you will need a Schengen visa if you are a citizen of a nation that is not a member of the EU or EEA. With a Schengen visa, you may travel to and within the Schengen Area, which is made up of Greece and 25 other European nations. You must submit your application to the Greek embassy or consulate in your country of residence in order to get a Schengen visa. It is crucial to apply well in advance of your intended trip since the application procedure often takes several weeks.

A valid passport or another form of identification, proof of lodging in Greece, evidence of sufficient funds to finance your stay, and a travel itinerary are all requirements for obtaining a Schengen visa. Depending on the reason for your visit, you could also be required to provide a medical certificate, evidence of travel insurance, and other papers. Even if your application is rejected, the visa application cost is non-refundable.

There are additional criteria for admission into Greece in addition to the visa requirements. All travelers must have a current passport that is valid for at least three more months after the date of their intended departure from Greece. You may need to secure extra permissions or documentation if you're going to Greece for a particular reason, like business or school.

Greece is a part of the European Union and the Schengen Area, thus the conditions for admission and visas are subject to change. This is an essential point to keep in mind. To make sure you have the necessary papers and can enter the nation without any problems, it is advised that you verify the most recent criteria before your trip.

It's Crucial to comprehend the visa and entrance procedures that are relevant to your nation of origin if you're arranging a vacation to Greece. Visitors from the EU, EEA, and Switzerland do not need a visa to enter Greece; however, travelers from other nations must apply for a Schengen visa. Depending on the reason for their trip, all visitors must have a current passport and fulfill extra entrance criteria. To prevent any problems at the border, it's crucial to review the most recent rules before you go.

Chapter 2: Essential Travel Tips for Greece

Understanding Greek Culture and Etiquette, Language and Currency

Greece has a long and varied history of linguistic diversity. The majority of the population speaks Greek, which is the official language of the country. With a history spanning more than 3,000 years, it is also one of the oldest languages in existence. Greek is an Indo-European language with a distinctive alphabet of its own.

There are several additional languages spoken in Greece in addition to Greek. Turkish, Albanian, and Macedonian are a few of them.

English is extensively spoken in several places, notably on islands and in tourist hotspots.

It's a good idea to learn some fundamental Greek words before traveling to Greece so you can connect with the locals. This may enhance your visit and help you have a better understanding of the local way of life. It will demonstrate to locals that you are making an attempt to connect with them in their language, which is often welcomed, even if you simply learn a few basic words.

There are several methods to converse with locals in English if you don't speak Greek well. As was already noted, English is a common language in tourist regions, and you'll discover that many people are at ease using it. Also, there are several menus and signage in both Greek and English in tourist locations.

It's crucial to keep in mind, too, that English may not be as extensively spoken outside of tourist hotspots. This is especially true in the nation's more rural or outlying regions. To facilitate communication with people in these locales, it might be useful to have a phrasebook or translation app on your phone.

There has been an effort in recent years to encourage tourists visiting Greece to study the Greek language. You may learn the fundamentals of the language and improve your ability to converse with locals by enrolling in one of the many organizations that provide language classes exclusively for visitors. If you want to remain in the nation for a lengthy amount of time or want to fully immerse yourself in the culture, these courses may be very beneficial.

Greek is the country's official language, however, English is also often spoken in tourist areas. Although it might be useful, learning some fundamental Greek words is not necessary for travel. It's also crucial to be mindful that English may not be as extensively spoken outside of tourist hotspots, so it's a good idea to have a phrasebook or translation app with you. Nevertheless, travelers to Greece shouldn't be too concerned about the language barrier since there are numerous resources available to assist you to speak with locals. In addition, this guide will provide some helpful Greek words and phrases.

The Euro is the recognized currency in Greece (EUR). The exchange rate between the US dollar (USD) and the euro (EUR) as of February 2023 is around 1 USD to 0.86 EUR. Exchange rates might vary, so it's always a good idea to check the current rate before flying. It's crucial to keep in mind that. 19 nations in the European Union utilize the euro, one of the most commonly used and acknowledged currencies in the world.

Coins are available in the following denominations: 1, 2, 5, 10, 20, and 50 cents, as well as €1 and €2 coins. The euro is split into 100 cents. The notes are available in the following denominations: 5, 10, 20, 50, 100, 200, and 500 euros. It is important to note that, while no longer being produced, the €500 banknote is still valid for use in transactions.

To guarantee you obtain the best exchange rates, it is advised to exchange money at authorized exchange offices, banks, or ATMs. Avoid doing your currency exchange at hotels, tourist businesses, or street sellers since they often impose greater costs and provide less advantageous exchange rates.

Value Added Tax (VAT) should be taken into account while visiting Greece. In many nations, including Greece, there is a tax called VAT that is tacked on to the cost of products and services. The cost of the majority of products and services in Greece includes the usual rate of VAT, which is 24%. Food, literature, and medical supplies are examples of things that are subject to a lower rate of VAT, which is levied at a rate of 13%. The VAT is completely free from several products, including exports and specific financial services.

It's essential to confirm whether or not VAT is included in the price before making a purchase in Greece. The price may sometimes be advertised without VAT, in which case you will be required to pay an extra 24% at the time of purchase. Tourists may be able to shop tax-free at certain establishments and then claim the VAT back when they depart the country. You will need to provide your passport and make a minimum purchase amount to be eligible for tax-free shopping.

In Greece, the majority of major credit cards are readily accepted, especially in touristy locations, lodgings, and dining establishments. Nonetheless, it's still a good idea to keep some cash on hand for minor purchases and as a backup, in case there are problems with your card. In Greece, ATMs are widely dispersed and a practical means to withdraw money in euros.

It is crucial to remember that Greece just had a financial crisis, which brought about considerable economic instability and uncertainty. Yet, the nation has made efforts to stabilize its economy, and things have much improved recently. Even so, tourists should proceed with care while carrying cash and exchanging it, as well as keep an eye on their surroundings, especially in busy places.

In Greece, the euro is a commonly used and reliable currency, so visitors shouldn't have any issues using it while they're there. To receive the best conversion rates, it's vital to use official exchange offices or ATMs, and it's also a good idea to carry extra cash in case your card stops working. Travelers should use care while carrying and exchanging money, be aware of their surroundings, and exhibit caution whenever they are in a strange nation to guarantee a safe and pleasurable journey.

The Architecture of Ancient Greece

Ancient Greek architecture is known for its splendor, accuracy, and ongoing impact on Western architecture. It is distinguished by the use of basic geometric shapes like the column and pediment as well as the emphasis on symmetry, balance, and harmony. Some of the most recognizable and lasting buildings in history, such as the Parthenon, the Temple of Olympian Zeus, and the Theater of Epidaurus, were built by Greek architects using these principles.

The Archaic era (750–480 BCE), the Classical period (480–323 BCE), and the Hellenistic period are the three different periods of Greek architecture (323-31 BCE). Different styles and methods, which reflect the political, social, and cultural shifts of the era, define each period.

Greek architecture during the Archaic era was primarily distinguished by the use of wood and mud brick. Temples were straightforward rectangular buildings with a single chamber, known as the cella, that contained the statue of the god to whom the temple was devoted. A colonnade of wooden columns often encircled the cella, offering support and shade. The Temple of Artemis in Corfu and the Temple of Hera in Olympia are two examples of this style of construction.

Greek architecture underwent a paradigm shift throughout the Classical era as stone and marble use increased. The development of the Doric, Ionic, and Corinthian orders—distinct forms of column design—marks this time period. The Doric order, which had a plain capital and no base, was the most straightforward and austere. The Ionic order was more ornamental, with a scroll-like capital and a fluted shaft. The most ornate order has a bell-shaped capital with acanthus leaves on it that were characteristic of the Corinthian style.

The Parthenon, a temple to the goddess Athena on the Acropolis in Athens, is the most well-known example of Classical Greek architecture. With eight columns on the east and west sides and seventeen columns on the north and south, the colonnade of the Parthenon is an illustration of the Doric order. The temple is ornamented with intricately carved metopes and friezes that represent episodes from Greek mythology.

The complexity and variety of Greek architecture increased throughout the Hellenistic era. Around this time, architects started experimenting with novel shapes and patterns, leading to the development of the Corinthian order. Also, they made use of modern architectural materials like colored stone and glass. The Theater of Epidaurus, a masterwork of classical acoustics, and the Temple of Olympian Zeus, which took over 700 years to finish, are two examples of Hellenistic architecture.

From the Renaissance to the present, Greek architecture has had a significant impact on Western architecture. Several of the concepts and methods used in Greek architecture, like the use of columns and the importance of symmetry and proportion, are being used today. Ancient Greek architecture is among the most significant and long-lasting examples of human innovation, and it serves as a tribute to the eternal beauty and force of human creation.

Byzantine Art and Architecture in Greece

The Eastern Roman Empire's aesthetic and architectural traditions, which persisted from the fourth century AD until Constantinople's fall in 1453, are referred to as Byzantine art and architecture. Greek art and culture, as well as those of other Eastern Mediterranean nations, were greatly influenced by Byzantine architecture and art. The Byzantine Empire was renowned for its beautiful cathedrals, imposing public structures, and decorative arts, such as linens, mosaics, and icons.

The creation of the church as a monumental architectural form is one of Byzantine art and architecture's most important contributions to Greece. Churches were often constructed during the Byzantine era in the shape of a cross, with a substantial central dome supported by four columns. A crucial component of Byzantine design, the central dome would be imitated in the following eras, especially the Ottoman Empire. Frescoes and intricate mosaics were often used to embellish churches, covering the interior walls and ceilings.

Some of the most important works of Byzantine art and architecture may be found in Thessaloniki, a city in northern Greece. One of Greece's biggest and most spectacular Byzantine churches is the Church of Saint Demetrios, which was constructed in the seventh century. It has a narthex, a series of galleries, and side chapels in addition to a central dome. Beautiful paintings and mosaics that portray incidents from the life of Saint Demetrios, the city's patron saint, are used to decorate the church's interior.

The Monastery of Hosios Loukas, which is situated in the highlands of central Greece, is another significant example of Byzantine art and architecture. Two churches and a refectory are among the well-preserved Byzantine monuments located at the monastery, which dates back to the 10th century. One of the best specimens of

Byzantine architecture in Greece is the Katholikon, the bigger of the two churches. It has a sizable central dome with gorgeous mosaics and frescoes that is supported by four columns.

Byzantine art is renowned for its decorative arts, such as icons, linens, and metalwork, in addition to its magnificent architecture. In Byzantine culture, icons—religious pictures painted on wooden panels—were a significant type of art. Many Byzantine icons still exist today and may be seen in Greek churches and museums. Some of the most well-known Byzantine mosaics and frescoes, in addition to a number of exquisite icons, may be seen at the Monastery of Daphni, which is not far from Athens.

Later creative traditions in Greece and other Eastern Mediterranean nations were greatly influenced by Byzantine art and architecture. The Byzantine Empire placed a strong emphasis on churches as monumental structures and placed an emphasis on ornamental arts, both of which had a lasting influence on the cultural environment of the area. Today, Byzantine art and architecture remain a significant component of Greece's cultural legacy and continue to serve as a source of inspiration for designers and artists throughout.

Modern Greek Art and Architecture

The rich and varied cultural history that has developed over the ages is reflected in modern Greek art and architecture. Greek art and architecture have been affected by a variety of styles, methods, and concepts from the ancient and Byzantine eras to the present.

Traditional and modern features are combined to create modern Greek architecture. The topography and climate of the nation have influenced architectural design, and it is typical to employ local resources such as stone, wood, and marble. International architectural movements like modernism and post-modernism have also impacted many contemporary Greek architects.

The Athens Olympic Sports Complex, which was constructed in preparation for the 2004 Olympic Games, is one of the most renowned instances of contemporary Greek architecture. The complex's main stadium, an indoor arena, and swimming pool were all created by a group of Greek architects. The complex has a modern style influenced by the architecture of ancient Greece, with crisp lines and straightforward forms that call to mind the classical era.

The Stavros Niarchos Foundation Culture Center in Athens is another illustration of contemporary Greek design. Renzo Piano, a well-known architect, created the center, which has a park, an opera theater, and a library. The center's architecture was motivated by the Greek countryside, and it has a sizable canopy for shade and sun protection.

Greek modern art is similarly varied, including both more modern forms and methods with elements of the nation's rich cultural background. Greek painters were affected by European modernism at the beginning of the 20th century, and many of them embraced movements like expressionism and cubism.

Yannis Tsarouchis, a prominent figure in contemporary Greek art, is well-known for his vivid and emotive paintings. Tsarouchis was active from the 1930s through the 1980s, and his work is distinguished by his use of mythical themes and motifs as well as brilliant colors.

Nikos Engonopoulos, a key figure in the surrealist movement in Greece, is another notable artist. The paintings of Engonopoulos are renowned for their vividness and imagination, which frequently include surreal and dreamy themes.

Greek contemporary art is also growing, with many artists innovating and producing one-of-a-kind pieces by combining both traditional and modern inspirations. Kostas Tsoklis is a well-known artist who creates immersive, interactive works using digital and multimedia methods.

The rich cultural past of the nation as well as more modern styles and methods continue to have a significant impact on modern Greek art and architecture. Greek art and architecture represent the nation's distinct personality and continual progress, from the Athens

Olympic Games Complex to the works of Yannis Tsarouchis and Nikos Engonopoulos.

Packing Tips for Greece

Greece is a well-liked tourist destination because of its fascinating history, lovely beaches, and breathtaking scenery. Yet, there are a few things to keep in mind while preparing for a vacation to Greece to make sure you're comfortable and ready for whatever experiences await you.

Priority one while packing is to consider the weather. Greece has hot, dry summers and moderate, rainy winters due to the influence of the Mediterranean. Pack light clothes made of breathable materials, such as cotton or linen, if you are going in the summer. To remain cool in the heat, try wearing shorts, t-shirts, or sundresses. You should carry a light sweater or shawl to cover your shoulders if required since certain religious sites in Greece have dress requirements.

Pack layers if you're visiting Greece in the winter or during one of the off-peak seasons. Due to the fact that temperatures might change throughout the day, it is wise to pack a variety of lightweight and heavier clothing alternatives. In the evenings, a lightweight jacket, cardigan, or scarf may be very helpful for staying warm.

With the amount of walking you'll be doing, it's crucial to wear comfortable shoes. Leave the high heels at home since Greece is a nation with plenty of rough terrain and cobblestone streets. Instead, choose a pair of sturdy shoes or comfy sandals that can withstand the miles you'll be walking.

Pack a few extra necessities in addition to your usual clothes and shoes. You must use sunscreen since the Greek sun may be quite intense. For hydration and UV protection, a hat, sunglasses, and a reusable water bottle may all be helpful.

It's a good idea to keep in mind your planned activities while you're packing for Greece. Pack a swimsuit, beach towel, and flip-flops if you want to spend a lot of time at the beach. A daypack might be helpful for carrying water, food, and other necessities if you want to do a lot of touring.

Lastly, it's critical to remember your airline's baggage policies. When you begin packing, be sure to verify the weight and size limits that the majority of airlines have on checked and carry-on bags. For day trips or excursions, it's also a good idea to have a small bag or backpack.

Greece demands specific preparation for the weather, activities, and cultural expectations. You can be sure that you're ready for all the experiences Greece has in store for you by bringing lightweight, comfortable clothes, comfy shoes, and necessary goods like sunscreen and a reusable water bottle.

Getting Around Greece: Transportation Options

Greece's public transportation system is surprisingly simple and effective for getting about. The reverse is true in Greece, contrary to the myth that public services there and in other Southern European nations are ineffective or never work well.

Greek railroads, ferries, and buses all follow regular schedules with few cancellations or delays. Very dependable, they can and will transport you wherever you wish to go in Greece.

How should you utilize Greece's public transportation options to go around one of the most stunning nations in the Mediterranean?

You will learn all you need to know about traveling in this section!

Domestic flights

Olympic Air and Aegean Airlines are the two primary domestic airlines in Greece. Although Sky Express and Astra Airlines (in

Thessaloniki) handle some charter flights during the summer, they manage the majority of domestic flights.

Greece has 42 airports that are open to the public, 15 of which are international and 27 domestic. If money were no issue, you could easily fly throughout all of Greece in a few hours!

Every airport that operates as an international airport will offer direct international flights that will take you straight to that area, skipping Athens, especially during peak season. Therefore, for instance, if you wish to skip Athens altogether and go straight to Mykonos or Santorini (Thera), you may.

While all domestic airports are open during the peak travel season, some of them are closed during the off-peak. This implies that alternative modes of transportation, such as ferries, will be required to reach certain islands or specific sites.

Like with other airlines, it is best to purchase your tickets as soon as possible since you will have a greater selection, pay less, and have more flexibility in selecting the day and time of your journey. Check all of the limits included with your tickets, including baggage and carry-on restrictions, since you can incur additional fees or even be denied boarding if you don't.

I suggest utilizing Skyscanner to quickly book your ticket, and compare costs, journey times, and more.

Ferries

In Greece, there are many distinct types of ferries, each with unique features and attributes. They operate as part of a vast, adaptable, and intricate network of private ferry firms that serve every island and port in Greece.

There are three different ferry types available:

The typical multi-deck cars-and-passengers ferry. The least expensive ticket is for deck seats, and there are often two or three classes plus cabins available for booking. While these boats go at the slowest speeds, they are the most dependable in severe weather. Choose them if you get seasick since they wobble the least when at sea.

Smaller ferries are hydrofoils. They go by the name "Flying Dolphins." There's not much space to walk about and the seating is similar to an aircraft. While they are very fast watercraft, they are also often vulnerable to bad weather and are readily grounded. Also, if you are prone to seasickness, they may not be very understanding. These may be found at the ports that link the islands in the same cluster.

The quickest and most technologically sophisticated ferries are catamarans. They are sometimes referred to as "Flying Cats" or "Sea Jets." There are often lounges and other facilities aboard, and some can transport vehicles. They often cost the most money as well.

Here, you may also discover caiques, which are simple, traditional boats used to ferry passengers over small distances to another island or around an island. They often have no restrooms, simply outside sitting on rough wooden benches and will swing a lot. They only carry a small number of people each time. Yet, they are fantastic for beautiful and enjoyable sailing.

With the exception of the Ionian Islands, all of the major island groups including Crete may be reached from Athens through the ports of Piraeus and Rafina. Lavrion, which is nearer to Athens and more effective for some of the islands since it is closer to them, is another option.

The ports of Patra, Igoumenitsa, and Kyllini link the Ionian Islands to the mainland. Some boats allow you to purchase a ticket just before boarding, even during peak season, but it's not a good idea to take that chance! The best course of action is to make an advance ticket purchase, preferably online. You may accomplish that by using Ferryhopper, which offers you the chance to compare and choose from all of the available routes and tickets.

It is wise to be at the port a few hours before the boat is scheduled to arrive. Two hours in advance could be preferable if it's a typical vehicle-and-passenger ferry, particularly if you want to bring your car with you. In this method, you may get on the plane quickly and skip most of the subsequent lines. Have a copy of your ticket and passport wherever you can quickly reach them in case the boat crew or port officials want to see them.

Trains

A great way to unwind, relax, and take in the stunning landscape is to travel throughout mainland Greece by rail. In Greece, trains are hygienic, dependable, and swift. Consider that the train travel from Athens to Thessaloniki takes around 4 hours to give you an idea of the timeframes.

The Greek railway company, Trainose, is in charge of running the trains in Greece. Both city trains and railways linking Greek cities are available. The Intercity Network is the quickest of them. It links Athens to the Peloponnese, Chalkida, Volos City, Central Greece, and Northern Greece (Kiato, Corinth, and Patras).

The railway from Diakofto to Kalavryta, the Pelion steam train, and the train from Katakolo to Ancient Olympia are three examples of "tourism lines" that are also provided by the Intercity Network and have significant cultural value for the Greeks. All three itineraries provide breathtaking scenery, and each one includes important cultural sites. Check the timetables and make reservations in advance if you're interested in using these lines, which are often open during the summer and on national holidays.

Odontotos rack railway Diakopto –Kalavrita

Seats are available in first class and economy on intercity trains. The first-class seats provide extra privacy and a foldable table. Also, they provide you with extra storage and legroom. Although having less privacy, economy-class chairs are broad and comfy at the shoulders.

While it is possible to purchase tickets at the station, it is not advisable to do so at the busiest times of the year. On the Trainose website or via their mobile application, you may purchase tickets online.

The KTEL buses

KTEL buses make up the majority of the buses that link all of the Greek cities. They provide affordable, effective transportation all around Greece. Local and intra-regional buses are the two different categories of KTEL buses.

Intra-regional buses are those that travel on key thoroughfares to link cities within a region. Regional roads, not highways, are used by the local ones to link the many settlements in a region. Local KTEL buses may be found all across the island and in locations with concentrations of interesting villages.

Sadly, there isn't a single website that compiles all KTEL routes. You could locate the websites that provide information by searching on Google for "KTEL" and the area you are interested in. For instance, every KTEL bus operating in Attica is listed on the "KTEL Attikis" website. KTEL buses often run the same route throughout the day, however, reservations are not necessary.

The majority of interregional buses arrive at the city's two main KTEL stations, Liosion station, and Kifissos station. Buses from Athens to Thessaloniki in the north and the Peloponnese in the south utilize the stations at Liosion and Kifissos, respectively.

These are a few of Greece's most well-known Ktel buses:

- **Ktel Attikis:** you can use this to go to Sounio
- **Ktel Thessalonikis:** if you are going Thessaloniki by bus
- **Ktel Volos:** if you are going to visit Pelion or taking boat to the Sporades islands

- **Ktel Argolidas:** If you are going to visit Nafplio, Mycenae, and Epidaurus.
- **Ktel Fokidas:** If you are going to visit the archaeological site of Delphi
- **Ktel Ioanninon:** If you want to visit Zagorohoria and Ioannina
- **Ktel Mykonos:** Public transport around the island
- **Ktel Santorini:** Public transport around the island
- **Ktel Milos**: Public transport around the island
- **Ktel Naxos :** Public transport around the island
- **Ktel Paros:** Public transport around the island
- **Ktel Kefalonia:** Public transport around the island
- **Ktel Corfu:** Public transport around the island
- **Ktel Rhodes**: Public transport around the island
- **Ktel Chania (Crete):** Public transport around the Chania area

Public transport in Athens

The train station in Athens

This should have a separate section for Athens. Not only because Athens is the capital of Greece, but also because it has a complex public transportation system that you will encounter unless you fly directly to the islands or to Thessaloniki.

To get about the sizable city, one may utilize buses, the subway (or metro), trains, trams, and even trolleys.

The railroad line, which links Piraeus with Kifissia, an Athens suburb, is the city's oldest. On the railway maps seen at train stations, it is also referred to as "the green line" and is labeled with the color green. From 5 am till midnight, trains operate.

The "blue" and "red" lines of the Athens metro extend the "green" line farther and go to Syntagma, the Acropolis, and Monastiraki, respectively. The trains operate on these most recent lines from 5:30 am to midnight.

The picturesque beaches of the Saronic Gulf may be seen when touring Athens on the city's tram. The red tram line from Syntagma Square goes to the Peace and Friendship Stadium; alternatively, you may take the blue line from that location to Voula or the Peace and Friendship Stadium.

Athens metro

There are bus stops located all across Athens, and the buses (which include trolleys) are generally blue and white in color. Use the tools on the dedicated site to locate it so you'll know which bus route to take while you explore Athens. The buses are available from 5 am till midnight, the same as the trains. The airport is nonetheless connected to Syntagma Square, the Athens KTEL stations, and Piraeus by a few unique 24-hour service buses.

You may get an anonymous ATH.ENA card from one of the merchants at any Athens railway station to use to make a reservation. This card may be filled with a single price for all modes of public transportation (train, metro, tram, trolley) for 90 minutes (1,20 euros), a 24-hour or 5-day pass, or a specific airport ticket. There is also a special 3-day tourist ticket that includes a 2-way ticket to the airport as well as a 3-day pass for all public transportation. You may see a list of the costs and access options here. If you adhere to the guidelines on the official website, you may also issue your card online.

Taxis

Last but not least, you may take a cab anywhere in Athens or even across cities. Taxis are yellow in Athens (they are often various colors in other cities), and you may hail one by raising your hand so the driver can see you as they pass. As an alternative, you may hail a taxi from locations where they are waiting in line and parking their cars. There is no official map of these "taxi piazzas," as they are known. The best way to find them is to ask the locals.

The best and safest method to use a taxi, however, is via an app like Taxi Beat or Taxiplon, which will give you an estimate of the cost for the journey you want, will display the ID of the vehicle you intend to use and will direct the taxi to your location. If you find yourself in a region with few cabs, this is extremely practical.

Keep in mind that the set cost of the travel from the airport to Athens is 38 euros during the day and 54 euros at night.

Ticket discounts

If you are a student (so be sure to have your student ID available!), are over 65, or qualify for another discount, you may be eligible. Nevertheless, you need a customized ATH.ENA card, which necessitates some documentation, to be able to get a discount on Athens' public transportation.

Children under the age of six often ride for free on public transit, but always check before you board.

There you have it, then! That is all there is to know about Greek public transportation. To get around it like a pro, all you have to do is do your research beforehand, reserve tickets when you can, and show up there to deal with everything else a little early.

Travel Insurance and Other Essential Travel Tips

Each overseas journey should take travel insurance into account, but it is particularly crucial when visiting a country like Greece. Although Greece is a typically secure and friendly destination for travelers, unforeseen circumstances may nevertheless occur, including minor medical difficulties, airline cancellations, and theft. These types of dangers may be reduced by purchasing travel insurance.

The ability of travel insurance to pay for unforeseen medical costs is one of its main advantages. Greece has a solid public health system, but visiting patients may have to pay more for care. Travel insurance may assist with the expense of medical care, including hospitalization, doctor's fees, and a prescription if you become sick or get hurt while visiting Greece.

Protection against trip interruption or cancellation is another benefit of travel insurance. If you have spent a lot of money on your vacation, this might be very crucial. Travel insurance may assist you in recovering part of your expenses if unexpected circumstances, such as a family emergency or a natural catastrophe, cause you to postpone or cancel your trip.

The ability to cover lost or stolen belongings, such as your passport and other vital papers, is another advantage of having travel insurance. Theft may occur everywhere, but it can be more upsetting when it does so in a foreign place. With travel insurance, you may get aid in replacing critical papers as well as monetary reimbursement for lost or stolen belongings.

It's crucial to thoroughly study the terms and conditions of the policy before selecting travel insurance for Greece so that you are aware of what is and is not covered. The coverage you get under certain plans may be limited by exclusions or limits. For instance, some insurance may not cover certain hobbies, such as high-risk or extreme sports. Others could place restrictions on the amount of coverage offered for certain kinds of costs.

It's also crucial to think about how much travel insurance will cost and how that will fit into your budget. Although it may be tempting to choose the least expensive choice, it's crucial to be sure the insurance offers sufficient coverage for your requirements. Moreover, think about the policy's reputation for customer care and if it offers round-the-clock help in the event of an emergency.

While visiting Greece, it is a good idea to invest in travel insurance since it may help shield you and your assets from a variety of unforeseen circumstances. You may travel in comfort knowing that you are properly protected in this stunning and ancient nation by selecting insurance that offers comprehensive coverage and matches your budget.

It is important to obtain travel insurance if you are considering a trip to Greece. In the event of unplanned occurrences like medical crises, trip cancellations, or missing baggage, travel insurance may provide you peace of mind. It might be difficult to choose the best insurance company for your requirements, however, since there are so many of them. Here are some pointers for acquiring travel insurance for your Greek vacation.

Start with your existing insurance provider: Your current insurance provider, such as the firm that handles your health or homeowner's insurance, could also be able to supply you with travel insurance. Inquire with them first to see whether or not they provide travel insurance and, if not, whether or not they can suggest another supplier.

Compare providers: After determining your insurance requirements, contrast the choices offered by various suppliers. To make sure they match your requirements, check for their exclusions, deductibles, and coverage limitations. Consult reviews and get referrals from friends and family who have already purchased travel insurance.

Consider a specialized provider: Other companies that specialize in travel insurance could give more specialized coverage for things like adventurous travel or unexpected medical expenses. If you want to engage in any activity that may not be protected by ordinary insurance, take into account these providers.

Purchase your insurance as soon as possible: The moment you've chosen a supplier, get your insurance as quickly as you can. Several carriers provide "cancel for any reason" insurance, but you must acquire it quickly after making your reservation. You are more likely to have this coverage the sooner you get insurance.

Keep your documents with you: Keep your policy documentation with you when traveling after acquiring insurance. This will guarantee that you can reach them in an emergency. Make sure you are familiar with the claims procedure and have your insurance provider's contact information on availability.

For your trip to Greece, purchasing travel insurance is crucial. To get the best coverage for your requirements, start with your current insurance carrier and evaluate possibilities from multiple companies. Get insurance as soon as you can, and when traveling, keep your paperwork with you. You may enjoy your vacation to Greece with confidence if you have the appropriate travel insurance.

It is important to obtain travel insurance if you are considering a trip to Greece. In the event of unplanned occurrences like medical crises, trip cancellations, or missing baggage, travel insurance may provide you peace of mind. It might be difficult to choose the best insurance company for your requirements, however, since there are so many of them. Here are some pointers for acquiring travel insurance for your Greek vacation.

Start with your existing insurance provider: Travel insurance could also be available through your current insurer, such as your health or homeowner's insurance provider. First, ask them whether they provide travel insurance or if they can suggest a carrier.

Compare providers: After determining your insurance requirements, contrast the choices offered by various suppliers. To make sure they match your requirements, check for their exclusions, deductibles, and coverage limitations. Consult reviews and get referrals from friends and family who have already purchased travel insurance.

Consider a specialized provider: Other companies that specialize in travel insurance could give more specialized coverage for things like adventurous travel or unexpected medical expenses. If you want to engage in any activity that may not be protected by ordinary insurance, take into account these providers.

Purchase your insurance as soon as possible: The moment you've chosen a supplier, get your insurance as quickly as you can. Several carriers provide "cancel for any reason" insurance, but you must acquire it quickly after making your reservation. You are more likely to have this coverage the sooner you get insurance.

Keep your documents with you: Keep your policy documentation with you when traveling after acquiring insurance. This will guarantee that you can reach them in an emergency. Make sure you are familiar with the claims procedure and have your insurance provider's contact information on availability.

In conclusion, purchasing travel insurance is crucial for your trip to Greece. To get the best coverage for your requirements, start with your current insurance carrier and evaluate possibilities from multiple companies. Get insurance as soon as you can, and when traveling, keep your paperwork with you. You may enjoy your vacation to Greece with confidence if you have the appropriate travel insurance.

There are various additional crucial travel suggestions to bear in mind before visiting Greece, in addition to packing and insurance. Here are some important things to think about as you get ready for your trip:

Transportation: You may need to utilize a number of modes of transportation in Greece, from buses and trains to ferries and cabs, depending on where you're going. Researching the available local transportation choices beforehand can help you prepare for what to anticipate. If you want to visit rural regions or smaller towns, you may also want to think about hiring a vehicle.

Cash vs. credit: Despite the fact that a lot of places in Greece take credit cards, it's always a good idea to have some cash on hand, particularly if you want to go to more rural regions or smaller enterprises. To prevent your cards from being frozen due to fraud suspicion, you may also wish to let your bank know about your vacation intentions.

Respect local customs: Greece has a long history of cultural heritage, many of which are being followed today. While visiting churches or other religious locations, it's particularly vital for visitors to observe local clothing regulations and traditions. Wearing long trousers or skirts or covering your shoulders may be suitable in some situations. Also, it's common to say "Yassou" (Greek for "hello") and "Efharisto" (Greek for "thank you") when necessary.

Stay hydrated: Especially in the summer, Greece may become rather warm and sunny. Keep yourself hydrated, particularly if you want to go climbing or walking a lot. Bring a reusable water bottle with you, and fill it up as necessary at cafés or public fountains.

Stay safe: Greece is a generally safe nation, but it's a good idea to use basic care wherever you go. Keep your belongings nearby and pay attention to your surroundings, particularly in busy places or popular tourist destinations. Avoid strolling alone at night if you're traveling alone, and remain in well-lit, busy places.

Learn a few basic Greek phrases: Although many Greeks can speak English, it's always welcomed when tourists try to communicate in their native tongue. Think about picking up a few fundamental words like "Parakalo" (please), "Ne" (yes), and "Ohi" (no). It will not only make it easier for you to interact with locals, but it may also be a pleasant method to get to know their way of life.

You can make your vacation to Greece fun, safe, and stress-free by remembering this important travel advice. You can make the most of your stay in this beautiful and intriguing nation with a little planning and common sense.

Part II: Athens

Chapter 3: Exploring Athens

Top Attractions in Athens

Greece's capital city, Athens, is a veritable treasury of historical importance and history. For each visitor to Greece, Athens is a must-visit location because of its magnificent structures, historic sites, and cutting-edge attractions. The following are the top sights in Athens that you should not skip:

Acropolis: The most recognizable landmark in Athens and one of the most significant ancient archaeological sites in the whole world is the Acropolis. The Parthenon, the Erechtheion, and the Propylaea are just a few of the historic structures that call this place home.

A group of historic buildings known as the Acropolis is perched on a rocky outcrop in the middle of Athens. One of the most popular and well-known sights in the whole globe. The area has been a hub of religion and civilization for millennia and has been inhabited since the Neolithic era.

The Parthenon is the most well-known building on the Acropolis. It was originally a temple devoted to the goddess Athena, the protector deity of Athens when it was constructed in the 5th century BC. The Parthenon is recognized for its astounding size, symmetry, and beauty and was built from Pentelic marble. With no straight lines or perfect angles, the temple is a wonder of ancient engineering. Instead, to provide the illusion of perfection to the human eye, it was constructed with curved lines and softly sloping angles.

Another historic temple on the Acropolis is the Erechtheion. It was constructed in the fifth century BC and was dedicated to both Athena and Poseidon. The Porch of the Maidens, which has six caryatids—sculpted female figurines that serve as columns—is where the temple is most known. The well and olive tree that are located within the Erechtheion's boundaries are additional attractions.

The grand entrance to the Acropolis is the Propylaea. It was constructed in the fifth century BC and served as the site's entryway for both tourists and the Panathenaic procession, a large event held every four years in Athena's honor.

The Acropolis provides stunning vistas of Athens in addition to its historic buildings. Visitors may see the whole city, the Aegean Sea, the surrounding mountains, and the city itself from the summit of the rocky outcrop.

Each trip to Athens must include a stop at the Acropolis, and tourists should budget at least a few hours to spend there. To escape the crowds and the heat, it is advised to visit in the early morning or late afternoon. Also, as the site is fairly rough and steep in some places, it's necessary to wear comfortable shoes. Also, visitors should respect historic buildings by not touching or climbing on them.

Acropolis Museum: The Acropolis Museum, a work of architectural beauty nearby the Acropolis, is home to some of the most significant artifacts discovered there. Ancient Greek art and culture may be seen firsthand at the museum.

For anyone interested in ancient Greek history and culture, the Acropolis Museum in Athens is a must-see destination. The museum provides a distinctive and immersive experience that highlights the best specimens of ancient Greek art and architecture and is situated in the historic district of Makriyianni, only a few steps from the Acropolis.

Since its opening in 2009, the museum has grown swiftly to rank among Athens' top tourist destinations, drawing in millions of people yearly. The Parthenon, which can be seen from the museum's top level, is intended to be reflected in the spectacular glass facade of the building. The museum's interior is home to a sizable collection of Acropolis-related archaeological artifacts that are shown in a contemporary and interactive manner.

Sculptures, pottery, jewelry, and other objects from the Archaic, Classical, and Roman eras are shown at the museum. The Caryatids, the Parthenon frieze, and the spectacular pediments that formerly decorated the Parthenon are some of the most significant items on exhibit. The unique architecture and lighting of the museum make it simple to observe the fine details of these ancient items.

The Acropolis Museum also organizes a variety of temporary exhibitions that focus on various facets of ancient Greek civilization in addition to the permanent displays. The museum also provides visitors with further insights into the background and importance of the objects on the show via guided tours and audio guides available in a variety of languages.

In general, anybody interested in the history and culture of ancient Greece should visit the Acropolis Museum. It is a unique and remarkable experience that should not be missed during a trip to Athens because of its gorgeous architecture and top-notch displays.

National Archaeological Museum: The National Archaeological Museum is one of the most significant archaeological museums in the world and the biggest museum in Greece. It has a sizable collection of antiquity-era items, including frescoes, jewelry, ceramics, and sculptures.

Everyone interested in Greek history and archaeology must visit the National Archaeological Museum. The museum, which lies in the city's center, has a magnificent collection of objects from the almost 5,000-year history of ancient Greece.

The museum has a sizable collection of sculptures, ceramics, and frescoes that may be seen by visitors. These art pieces are grouped chronologically and date from the Neolithic to the Roman eras. The Mycenaean Collection, one of the most prominent displays, showcases an amazing collection of gold items that were found at Mycenae, the ancient city that formerly served as the hub of the Mycenaean civilization.

Additional attractions include the Cycladic Collection, which is devoted to the ancient Cycladic culture and has a spectacular collection of figures and ceramics, and the Bronze Collection, which displays a variety of bronze items, including swords, figurines, and vessels.

Visitors may benefit from a variety of educational and interactive activities, including seminars, guided tours, and lectures, in addition to the museum's enormous collection, all of which are intended to provide a more thorough knowledge of ancient Greek history and culture.

Anybody traveling to Athens should not miss the National Archaeological Museum, which provides a fascinating look into the lengthy and intricate history of Greece.

Plaka: Athens' Plaka is a historic district distinguished by its neoclassical buildings, ancient tavernas, and charming, winding lanes. There are several gift stores there, making it a nice spot to roam and explore.

For anybody who loves history and culture, Plaka is an area in Athens that they must visit. It is situated at the base of the Acropolis, and the lovely neoclassical structures that line its winding alleyways take tourists back in time to the 19th century. Visitors may explore the quaint stores and eateries that line the streets while taking in the gorgeous ambiance of the area.

The Ancient Agora, a market area from the sixth century BC, is one of Plaka's most well-known attractions. The Temple of Hephaestus and the Stoa of Attalos, among other ancient temples and monuments, are still visible to visitors. There is a museum in the Ancient Agora where tourists may see items from the location.

Traditional taverns in Plaka are also well-known for serving guests a taste of real Greek food. These tavernas provide a selection of traditional foods such as moussaka, souvlaki, and dolmades in addition to regional wines and alcoholic beverages. The open-air eating spaces, which are often adorned with plants and flowers, are where visitors may have their meals.

Plaka is a fantastic spot to go shopping for souvenirs in addition to its historical and gastronomic attractions. There are several stores in the area that offer authentically Greek goods including handcrafted jewelry, ceramics, and olive oil. Tourists may peruse the stores and purchase one-of-a-kind souvenirs to bring home as memories of their vacation to Athens.

A look into Athens' past and present may be had by tourists in the beautiful and scenic suburb of Plaka. For everyone visiting the Greek capital, it is a must-visit location because of its winding alleyways, neoclassical architecture, traditional tavernas, and distinctive boutiques.

Monastiraki Flea Market: The Monastiraki Flea Market, which is situated in the center of Athens, is a lively market where you can buy everything from vintage furniture to contemporary goods. The local culture may be experienced while shopping there.

One of the most well-known marketplaces in Athens is the Monastiraki Flea Market, which provides a distinctive shopping experience that is both traditional and contemporary. Due to its vibrant ambiance and a wide variety of goods, the market is a well-liked hangout for both residents and visitors.

The market is conveniently located in the historic Agora in the center of Athens and is accessible by bus or metro. The ideal time to come is in the morning when the booths are new and there are fewer visitors. It is open every day save Sunday.

Each of the market's divisions offers a distinct range of commodities. The most populated section is the central one, where you can discover a large variety of goods including apparel, jewelry, and mementos. This region is particularly well-known for its antique stores, which provide a range of one-of-a-kind and uncommon goods including antique coins, old books, and vintage timepieces.

There are a number of side streets and alleyways that are worth investigating in addition to the center area. Some places are less congested and provide a more laid-back shopping atmosphere. Local specialties like honey, olives, and spices are available here, along with handcrafted items and authentic Greek goods.

The Monastiraki Flea Market is a fantastic spot to discover the local culture in addition to shopping. The market is a fantastic site to learn about the city's past and present since it reflects the history and many influences of the city. Together with the market itself, there are a number of interesting historical sites nearby, including the Hadrian Library, the Roman Forum, and the old Agora.

A must-see location in Athens is the Monastiraki Flea Market, which provides a distinctive and exciting shopping experience that is both traditional and contemporary. The market is a terrific spot to get a taste of the local culture and enjoy all Athens has to offer because of its wide variety of goods, vibrant atmosphere, and rich cultural past.

Ancient Agora: Another significant archaeological monument in Athens is the Ancient Agora, which formerly served as the hub of the city's political and social life. The Church of the Holy Apostles, the Temple of Hephaestus, and the Stoa of Attalos are just a few of the historic structures that can be found there.

For history fans and anyone with a passion for ancient Greek culture, the Ancient Agora is a must-see sight. It served as the focal point for social, commercial, and political activity when Athens' life was at its center. The location, which originates in the sixth century BC, was where the Athenians' assembly met to discuss and vote on significant problems. Many governmental structures, commercial buildings, and religious places may be found inside the agora.

The Stoa of Attalos, a two-story colonnade that was rebuilt in the 1950s, is one of the Ancient Agora's most spectacular buildings. Once used to house stores and workshops, it now functions as a museum where a variety of items discovered in the agora are on exhibit. The museum is a veritable gold mine of ancient Greek art and culture, including artifacts like sculpture and ceramics alongside coins and jewelry.

The Temple of Hephaestus, one of Greece's best-preserved ancient temples, is another feature of the Ancient Agora. Its exquisite Doric columns and delicate carvings are a monument to the talent of ancient Greek builders and artists. Constructed in the 5th century BC, it was dedicated to the god of metals and workmanship.

In the Ancient Agora, the Church of the Holy Apostles is another important structure. It is a well-preserved example of Byzantine architecture and was constructed in the 10th century AD. The cathedral contains the grave of the Greek artist Aristeides and is decorated with stunning murals.

Other noteworthy locations in the Ancient Agora include the Tholos, a circular structure that may have served as a venue for meetings of the Prytaneis, the city's administrative authorities, and the Odeon of Agrippa, a tiny theater that was utilized for musical performances.

Everyone interested in history and culture must visit the Ancient Agora, which provides a fascinating look into everyday life in ancient Athens.

Lycabettus Hill: Athens' highest peak, Lycabettus Hill, provides breathtaking views of the city. It's a terrific location for hiking, relaxation, and watching the sunset.

Lycabettus Hill, sometimes referred to as Mount Lycabettus, is a hill that provides tourists with breathtaking panoramic views of the city and is situated in the center of Athens. The hill, which is 277 meters high, may be reached by a funicular train or on foot along a beautiful trail. The hill is a well-liked destination for both residents and visitors and is a wonderful spot to unwind and take in the breathtaking views.

Visitors will discover a lovely church honoring Saint George at the summit of the hill, which is a well-liked location for wedding ceremonies. Also, there is a restaurant where guests may dine or drink while admiring the magnificent views of the city.

Lycabettus Hill hikes are a well-liked adventure activity for individuals who want a little bit of challenge. The hiking path ascends through woodland from where it begins at the base of the hill. The well-marked route takes between 30 and 40 minutes to reach the summit. The climb is a really immersive experience because of the several vistas that give guests a glance of the city along the route.

A fantastic time to visit Lycabettus Hill is just before sunset when the sky is painted with pink and orange tones. Anybody visiting

Athens should take in the genuinely stunning view from the hill at this time of day.

For travelers visiting Athens, Lycabettus Hill is a magnificent destination. The panoramic views of the city are worth the effort whether you opt to trek up or ride the funicular train. Bring a camera so you may record the breathtaking views!

Syntagma Square: The Greek Parliament is located in Athens' central center, Syntagma Square. It's an excellent location to people-watch, have a beverage, and see the ceremonial changing of the guard.

The hub of Athens is the crowded public space known as Syntagma Square. It is a well-liked meeting spot for both residents and visitors. The Tomb of the Unknown Soldier, which is guarded by the Evzones, an elite ceremonial unit of the Greek military, is located in the middle of the plaza. A changing of the guard's event that is accompanied by a band and draws large throngs of onlookers takes place every hour.

The Greek Parliament building is located in Syntagma Square, together with the Tomb of the Unknown Soldier. To understand more about Greek history and culture, visitors may take a tour of the structure. The building is a stunning neoclassical construction that was constructed in the 19th century and has made a significant contribution to the political history of the nation.

A coffee or beverage is a terrific way to relax around Syntagma Square. The area is surrounded by various cafés and pubs that provide guests a chance to unwind while taking in the sights and sounds of the city. People-watching is also quite popular here since both residents and visitors walk through the area all day long.

In addition to being a significant location in terms of culture and history, Syntagma Square serves as a transit hub for Athens. Below the square lies a metro station that offers quick access to different sections of the city. The area is a good spot for travelers to begin or conclude their trips since buses and taxis also stop there.

Everyone visiting Athens should make sure to visit Syntagma Square. It is a well-liked destination for both tourists and residents due to its strategic position, historical value, and lively environment.

Temple of Olympian Zeus: Zeus, the ruler of the gods, was honored at the ancient temple known as the Temple of Olympian Zeus, which is still standing in the middle of Athens. Every history enthusiast should go to it since it is one of the biggest temples from antiquity.

The Olympieion sometimes referred to as the Temple of Olympian Zeus, is a beautiful ancient temple that is situated in the center of Athens. It was built in honor of Zeus, the supreme ruler of the gods, and was one of the biggest temples ever built.

The temple started being built in the sixth century BC, but it wasn't finished until the Roman era, more than 600 years later. In its height, the temple had 104 enormous columns that were around 17 meters tall apiece. Although just 15 columns are still intact, they are nonetheless awe-inspiring to see.

Visitors to the Temple of Olympian Zeus may tour the temple's remains and discover more about its importance and history. The temple was a crucial political and religious hub in ancient Athens and contributed significantly to the cultural legacy of the city.

Visitors may tour the neighboring Hadrian's Arch, which was constructed in 132 AD to commemorate the entrance of the Roman Emperor Hadrian to Athens, in addition to the spectacular remains.

The temple's old Greek remains are beautifully contrasted by the arch, a stunning example of Roman construction.

The Temple of Olympian Zeus is conveniently close to public transit and is situated in the center of Athens. The National Gardens and the Panathenaic Stadium are two places that visitors should plan to visit throughout their at least an hour-long exploration of the ruins.

For those who are interested in the history and architecture of ancient Greece, the Temple of Olympian Zeus is a must-see destination. An interesting and unforgettable visit to Athens is made possible by the spectacular remains, the neighboring Hadrian's Arch, and other historical locations.

Mount Pentelicus: A mountain outside of Athens called Mount Pentelicus is renowned for its magnificent marble, which was used to construct a number of the city's historic structures, notably the Parthenon. It is a wonderful location for hiking and seeing Greece's natural splendor.

In Greece's Attica area, not far from Athens, lies the beautiful natural landmark known as Mount Pentelicus. It is called for the

Pentelikon marble, which was used to construct a number of the city's historic structures and has been extracted from the mountain's quarries for generations. The mountain is a well-liked location for both nature lovers and outdoor enthusiasts due to its pure pine woods, breathtaking vistas, and hiking routes.

Hiking is one of the most well-liked pastimes on Mount Pentelicus. The mountain's summit is reached via a number of pathways, each of which provides a different vantage point of the surroundings. There is a path for every level of a hiker since they vary in intensity from simple to hard. Hikers will come across a variety of flora and animals along the journey, such as wildflowers, butterflies, and birds. Also, there are a number of picnic sites and viewpoint locations where guests may pause and take in the breathtaking views.

You may learn a lot about Athens' past and present by visiting Mount Pentelicus. The mountain's marble quarries have been in operation since antiquity, and tourists may still see signs of this business today. The ruins of a temple erected to worship the deity Pan are also accessible, along with a number of old quarries. The temple, which is situated on a mountain and provides breathtaking views of the surroundings, is said to have been utilized for religious activities.

Several more activities are available for individuals who wish to take in Mount Pentelicus's natural beauty without climbing. Several churches and monasteries may be found atop the mountain, notably the 11th-century Kaisariani Monastery. In addition, the region offers opportunities for rock climbing, mountain biking, and equestrian riding.

For anybody visiting Athens who enjoys both nature and history, Mount Pentelicus is a must-see location. It provides a distinctive glimpse of the people, culture, and natural beauty of Greece with its breathtaking vistas, hiking routes, and historic monasteries. Mount Pentelicus is the ideal location whether you're an outdoor enthusiast, a history nerd, or simply searching for a quiet getaway from the city.

In conclusion, Athens is a place with a rich history, a vibrant culture, and some of the most significant archaeological sites in the world. Whether your interests—history, art, or just getting a taste of the local life—Athens has plenty to offer. While visiting Athens, be sure to include these popular sights on your schedule.

Walking Tour of Historic Athens

The greatest way to see Athens is on foot. Having a rich history and cultural legacy, the best way to see many of the city's attractions is to stroll about and take in all of its sights and sounds. This historical Athens walking tour will take you to some of the city's most well-known attractions.

Syntagma Square: Syntagma Square, Athens' central plaza, is where the tour starts. Due to its convenient access to the rest of the city by public transportation, this is an excellent site to begin your trip. From here, you may wander along the plaza, see the ceremonial changing of the guard, and admire the stunning design of the Greek Parliament building.

Athens' Syntagma Square is a hive of activity and a fantastic place to start any walking tour of the city. The area, which is in the center of Athens, is surrounded by old buildings, shops, cafés, and restaurants, making it a fantastic site to experience the Greek way of life.

The Greek Parliament building, which can be seen on the east side of Syntagma Square, is one of the most well-known sights there. The stately neoclassical edifice, which houses the Greek Parliament, was built in the 19th century. The elite Greek Presidential Guard, known as the Evzones, performs in the changing of the guard ritual, which is broadcast live to spectators every hour on the hour.

The fountain in the middle of Syntagma Square is another well-liked destination there. Triton, the son of Poseidon, and other mythical sea animals are depicted in sculptures atop this 19th-century fountain. In the summer, people often stop by the fountain to cool down and snap pictures.

Many additional ancient structures can be seen around Syntagma Square, notably the opulent 5-star Hotel Grande Bretagne, which was built in the 19th century. Throughout the years, the hotel has welcomed a number of well-known visitors, including Madonna, Nelson Mandela, and Winston Churchill.

National Gardens: Go to the National Gardens, a stunning park in the middle of the city, from Syntagma Square. This is a wonderful location to unwind and take in Greece's natural beauty. There are several ponds, a small zoo, and lovely trees and flowers throughout the grounds.

The Royal Palace grounds were previously included in the National Gardens, which were established in the middle of the 19th century. The 15.5-hectare-sized gardens are accessible to the public every day from sunrise to nightfall. A picnic on the grass, a leisurely walk around the gardens, or a respite from the bustle of the city are all options for visitors.

The Botanical Museum is one of the National Gardens' most well-liked attractions. The museum includes a herbarium, a library, and a collection of plants from all over Greece and the Mediterranean. Except on Mondays, the museum is open every day and entrance is free.

The little zoo, which is home to a variety of animals including peacocks, ducks, and goats, is another noteworthy feature of the National Gardens. Families should visit the zoo, particularly if their children are small.

The National Gardens include a zoo, a botanical museum, a number of ponds, a playground, and a café. The numerous seats that are scattered around the gardens allow visitors to unwind, take in the cityscape, and have a coffee or a snack at the café.

The National Gardens are a tranquil haven in the middle of Athens and provide a much-needed break from the clamor and mayhem of the city. Before continuing your walking tour of old Athens, it's a terrific spot to get your energy back.

Zappeion Hall: Next, go to Zappeion Hall, a stunning neoclassical structure that is often utilized for events and exhibits. The edifice, a stunning specimen of neoclassical architecture, was built in the late 19th century.

For everyone interested in architecture and history, Zappeion Hall at the National Gardens is a must-visit location. Theophil Hansen, a Danish architect, created the structure, which was finished in 1888. The first modern Olympic Games, which were held in Athens in 1896, were the reason it was first constructed.

The structure's exterior is made up of Corinthian columns and pediments, reflecting the building's strong Greek architectural influences. The spectacular center hall is often utilized for exhibits, performances, and other events. Many significant pieces of art are also housed there, one of which is a bronze figure of George Washington created by the Danish artist Bertel Thorvaldsen.

Take a guided tour of Zappeion Hall to discover more about the history and architecture of the structure. The center hall, the tiny hall, and the gardens are all covered throughout the excursions, which run for around 45 minutes.

Zappeion Hall is a well-liked location for residents to unwind and mingle in addition to serving as a venue for events and exhibits.

Visitors may stroll around the lovely grounds surrounding the building and have a meal or a cup of coffee at one of the many adjacent cafés and eateries.

Everyone with an interest in architecture, history, or art should visit Zappeion Hall. Its stunning architecture and historical history make it an intriguing destination to discover, and its setting in the National Gardens makes it a tranquil and restful oasis in the middle of the city.

Panathenaic Stadium: Make your way to the Panathenaic Stadium, which hosted the first modern Olympic Games in 1896, from Zappeion Hall. The Panathenaic Games were held at this antiquity's 4th-century BC stadium. In the late 19th century, it underwent restoration, and now it is a well-liked tourist destination.

A stop on every walking tour of the city must include the Panathenaic Stadium, one of Athens' most well-known sites. The Panathenaic Games, which were staged in honor of the goddess Athena, were held at the stadium, which was constructed completely of marble in the fourth century BC. Other significant occasions, including sporting competitions, musical concerts, and political rallies, were also held at the stadium.

Throughout the years, the stadium lost usage and was finally abandoned. It was renovated in the late 19th century in time for Athens to host the first modern Olympic Games in 1896. Since then, the stadium has hosted a number of subsequent Olympic Games, including the 2004 Games, and it continues to host a number of athletic and cultural events.

A guided tour of the stadium gives visitors access to both the building itself and a museum that chronicles the history of the Olympic Games. The stadium is a stunning example of classical Greek architecture and a fantastic location to learn about the Olympic Games history and link to Greece.

Visitors may see the grandstands, which are completely constructed of marble and have room for 50,000 people, as they go around the stadium. The field is also surrounded by a track that is composed of a particular kind of dirt to protect the marble surface. Even walking on the track allows visitors to experience what it might have been like to participate in the ancient games.

The Panathenaic Stadium is notable for its historical value but is also a wonderful location to enjoy Athens' natural beauty. Visitors may see panoramic views of the city, including the Acropolis and Lycabettus Hill, from the stadium's highest point. Visitors may enjoy a leisurely walk in the nearby park, which is surrounded by beautiful vegetation, while they are at the stadium.

A fantastic stop on a walking tour of old Athens is the Panathenaic Stadium. It is a must-see sight for every traveler to Athens because of its impressive architecture, rich history, and breathtaking vistas.

Temple of Olympian Zeus: After that, go to the ancient temple of Olympian Zeus, which is devoted to Zeus, the ruler of the gods. One of the biggest temples in ancient history, the temple was constructed in the sixth century BC.

In the center of Athens, there lies a magnificent ancient temple called the Temple of Olympian Zeus. The deity Zeus, the ruler of the gods in Greek mythology, is the subject of this temple, which was constructed in the sixth century BC. It took a long time to build, and it wasn't finished until the second century AD, long after its original architects had passed away.

Limestone, marble, and Pentelic marble were among the several kinds of stone used to construct the temple. It was a significant endeavor, with more than 100 marble columns that could reach heights of 17 meters. Sadly, only a handful of the original columns are still intact, but even so, they provide a taste of the grandeur of this old building.

The Temple of Olympian Zeus was constructed to symbolize the might and might of the Greek deities and to commemorate the

Greeks' triumph over the Persians in the Battle of Marathon. Since that construction was financed by tax dollars, the temple was also intended to stand for Athens' democratic government.

Despite its splendor, the temple gradually deteriorated, and most of the marble was removed and utilized in other structures. The temple was repaired and some of the columns were rebuilt during the Roman period. The temple was still in use up to the third century AD, when the spread of Christianity caused it to be abandoned.

In the Temple of Olympian Zeus today, tourists may stroll amid the surviving columns and take in the temple's immense grandeur and scope. A modest museum that exhibits a number of fascinating relics connected to the history of the temple is also located there. A statue of Emperor Hadrian, who supervised the temple's reconstruction during his rule, is one of the most intriguing relics.

Anybody interested in Greek mythology or ancient architecture must see the Temple of Olympian Zeus, a significant site in Athens' ancient past. To truly appreciate the temple's magnificence and history, visitors should set aside at least an hour.

Hadrian's Arch: Make your way from the Temple of Olympian Zeus to Hadrian's Arch, a stunning structure that was erected in the second century AD to mark the arrival of the Roman Emperor Hadrian.

A striking structure called Hadrian's Arch stands beside the Temple of Olympian Zeus. In celebration of the arrival of the Roman Emperor Hadrian in Athens, this marble arch was built in AD 131. It functioned as the entrance to the city and as a dividing line between the prehistoric and Roman portions.

The arch is a stunning illustration of Roman construction and has many decorative accents, such as reliefs and inscriptions. The reliefs show episodes from Greek mythology and history, such as Hercules' labors, Theseus' conflict with the Minotaur, and Athena's foundation of the city.

It is believed that the arch was once part of a bigger monument that stretched over both of the important ancient thoroughfares it sits at the crossroads of. Currently, it is a well-liked location for travelers to snap pictures while admiring the arch's complex architecture and rich history.

Tourists may pause here to take in the city views or continue their tour of old Athens after passing beneath the arch. The presence of the Roman Empire in Athens is attested to by Hadrian's Arch, which also serves as a reminder of the city's lengthy and intricate past.

Acropolis: Last but not least, a trip to Athens is not complete without a stop at the Acropolis. The Parthenon, the Erechtheion, and the Propylaea are just a few of the notable structures that can be seen within this historic stronghold. A history enthusiast must go to this sight.

A trip to Athens wouldn't be complete without viewing this majestic historic castle, which is known as the Acropolis. The Acropolis is home to numerous famous ancient Greek structures that have come to represent the pinnacle of ancient Greek culture. It is perched on a rocky hill overlooking the city.

The Propylaea, a grand entrance constructed in the fifth century BC, will be encountered as you ascend the twisting road toward the summit of the hill. It is an example of the ability and creativity of the ancient Greeks, and it has multiple columns and a great stairway.

The Parthenon, the most well-known structure on the Acropolis, is located beyond the Propylaea. The goddess Athena, the patron goddess of Athens, was honored during the construction of this historic temple in the fifth century BC. With its exquisite friezes representing episodes from Greek mythology and its precisely sized columns, the Parthenon is a marvel of ancient engineering and design.

The Erechtheion, another historic temple constructed in the fifth century BC, is located next to the Parthenon. This structure is famous for its unique design, which combines elements of the Ionic, Doric, and Corinthian architectural styles. The Porch of the Caryatids, a series of six female statues used as roof support columns, is another well-known feature of the Erechtheion.

The Temple of Athena Nike, a graceful temple constructed in the Fifth Century BC, and the Odeon of Herodes Atticus, a magnificent antique theater constructed in the Second Century AD, are just two of the many historic structures you will encounter as you tour the Acropolis.

You will be awed by the magnificence and beauty of these historic structures during your journey to the Acropolis, and you will have a greater understanding of the talent, craftsmanship, and inventiveness of the ancient Greeks. Anybody interested in ancient history, architecture, or culture must definitely visit the Acropolis.

You'll see some of the city's most well-known sights on this walking tour of ancient Athens, which will also give you a fantastic feel of the city's history and culture. Remember to pack a water bottle, wear comfortable shoes, and take your time seeing the city's various attractions.

Eating and Drinking in Athens

Athens is a city with a thriving culinary scene that offers a huge selection of mouthwatering traditional foods and beverages. There are a variety of alternatives to suit every taste, from formal dining to street cuisine. In Athens, try these dishes and beverages at least once:

Souvlaki: This meal, which includes grilled meat—typically pig, chicken, or lamb—served on a skewer or in a pita with tomato, onion, and tzatziki sauce, is perhaps the most well-known Greek food. Souvlaki stands can be found all throughout the city, and they're a terrific choice for a fast, inexpensive, and delectable dinner.

One of the most well-liked Greek meals, souvlaki is a favorite of both residents and visitors. It is a fast lunch or supper that is straightforward and tasty. Grilled pig, chicken, or lamb that has been marinated in a combination of olive oil, lemon juice, garlic, and herbs makes up souvlaki. After that, the meat is skewered and expertly cooked over an open flame, giving it a crisp outside and a succulent, soft inside.

There are many different methods to serve souvlaki. Serving it on a skewer, with chunks of beef alternating with onions, tomatoes, and sometimes peppers is one common method. Tzatziki sauce, a creamy dip prepared from Greek yogurt, cucumber, and garlic, is then given as a side with the skewer. It's a marriage made in heaven when the tangy tzatziki sauce is paired with the juicy, delicious meat.

Pita bread is a common container for souvlaki, which is another popular method to eat it. Warm pita bread is topped with fresh tomato, onion, and tzatziki sauce and wrapped over the grilled meat. The outcome is a satisfying lunch that is ideal for eating while on the move.

Athens is home to many souvlaki outlets, from busy markets to street corners. Locals often go there for a quick meal or a late-night snack after a night out. For tourists on a tight budget, souvlaki is a fantastic choice since it is both inexpensive and delicious.

A must-eat food while in Athens is souvlaki. You're sure to like the mouthwatering mix of grilled beef, fresh veggies, and tangy tzatziki sauce whether you eat it on a skewer or in pita bread.

Moussaka: This traditional Greek meal is cooked in the oven with layers of eggplant, ground beef, and béchamel sauce. For a sit-down lunch or supper, this rich and savory dish is ideal.

Greek comfort meal known as moussaka has gained popularity all over the globe. Typically, layers of sliced eggplant, minced meat (commonly lamb or beef), and a rich béchamel sauce make up this substantial dish. It is then cooked until the top is bubbling and brown, producing a meal that is rich in taste and ideal for colder times.

Moussaka comes in a wide variety of forms, each with its own distinctive characteristics depending on the location and household. Yet, the fundamental components and method of preparation remain the same.

The recipe starts with sliced, salted eggplant that has been cut to remove any extra moisture and bitterness. After being cleaned, the eggplant is either fried or roasted until brown and succulent. The minced beef is cooked until browned and aromatic with onion, garlic, and tomato paste. For added texture and taste, some moussaka recipes also incorporate other veggies like potatoes or zucchini.

A crucial element in the meal, the béchamel sauce adds a thick, creamy coating that helps bind the components together. The sauce is prepared by combining butter and flour in a skillet and whisking until paste forms. Then, gently whisk in the milk to get a smooth and velvety consistency. To give the sauce more taste, cheese is often added.

As each ingredient is ready, the moussaka is put together in a baking dish, first with an eggplant layer, then adding minced beef, then béchamel sauce. The last layer is the béchamel sauce, and this procedure is repeated until all the ingredients have been utilized. After that, the moussaka is roasted in the oven until the top is bubbling and brown.

With a side of salad or a piece of crusty bread, moussaka is often served as the main dish. It is often served at family get-togethers and special events since it is a pleasant and hearty meal that is ideal for colder weather.

Although moussaka is a traditional Greek dish, it has also gained popularity outside thanks to adaptations for other cuisines. For instance, a meal similar to this is often prepared in Turkey with ground beef, eggplant, and potatoes under the name "musakka," and in several Middle Eastern nations with eggplant, chickpeas, and tomato sauce under the name "maghmour."

There are several eateries and taverns in Athens that serve moussaka, and each one has its own spin on the traditional meal. To produce a distinctive taste, some areas could add more ingredients or other spices, while others might keep to the classic recipe.

Everybody visiting Athens should have moussaka, a wonderful and hearty meal. It's a meal that will satisfy any hunger thanks to its layers of soft eggplant, savory minced beef, and creamy béchamel sauce.

Greek Salad: With tomatoes, cucumbers, red onion, feta cheese, olives, and a sprinkle of olive oil and vinegar, this recipe is simple yet delicious. It's a light and healthful choice that is offered in practically all of the restaurants in Athens.

Greek salad, also known as horiatiki salad, is a locally famous meal that has gained popularity worldwide. It's a straightforward recipe that tastes great and is crafted with premium, fresh ingredients, making it ideal for sweltering summer days.

Ripe tomatoes, crisp cucumbers, thinly sliced red onions, crumbled feta cheese, Kalamata olives, and a basic dressing of olive oil and red wine vinegar make up the foundation of a Greek salad. Green peppers, capers, and fresh oregano are a few options. In most cases, the ingredients are placed on a dish, and drizzled with the dressing, rather than being combined.

In a Greek salad, the cucumbers are generally crisp and cooling, while the tomatoes are usually juicy and tasty. The richness of the tomatoes is sharply offset by the red onions, and the feta cheese provides a salty, acidic taste. Often cut into slices and pitted, Kalamata olives provide a salty taste that complements the other components.

Greek salads have a simple yet tasty dressing. It is seasoned with salt, pepper, and oregano and is prepared with extra virgin olive oil and red wine vinegar. A piece of crusty bread is often provided with the salad to soak up any surplus dressing, and the dressing is typically put to the salad just before serving.

Greek salad is a wonderful supper all by itself, but it also goes well with grilled fish, meat, or veggies. It's a tasty, wholesome, and nutritious alternative that is a wonderful way to obtain your recommended daily intake of veggies. It is also light and healthful.

Greek salad may be found in practically all restaurants in Athens, from low-key sidewalk cafés to upscale dining establishments. It's important to choose a restaurant that serves food made using local, fresh products since the quality of the ingredients might differ.

Traditional taverns and ouzeries are some of the greatest venues to have a Greek salad in Athens, where you can pair the salad with a glass of ouzo, the country's famed anise-flavored liquor.

For a light lunch or supper, a wonderful and healthful alternative is a Greek salad. It's a fantastic opportunity to sample Greek cuisine and the Mediterranean diet, which is renowned for its health advantages.

Gyro: Gyros, which are similar to souvlaki but prepared with meat grilled on a vertical rotisserie and served in a pita with tomato, onion, and tzatziki sauce, are a common fast food item in Greece. It's a delightful and satisfying alternative that's ideal for a fast snack.

The Greek delicacy known as gyros has spread around the globe and is now a common street snack. It is made out of rotisserie-cooked meat that is served in a pita with tomato, onion, and tzatziki sauce. Pork, chicken, lamb, or any mix of these meats may be used in gyros. The tasty and satisfying gyro is ideal for a fast dinner on the run.

The Middle East is where the gyro's origins may be found, where shawarma, a cuisine that is similar, was well-liked. Immigrants from the Middle East introduced the idea of cooking meat in a vertical rotisserie to Greece, and the cuisine developed into what is now known as gyro. In Greece, gyros first gained popularity in the 1920s and have since grown to be a treasured national dish.

Before being grilled on a vertical rotisserie, the meat used in gyros is often marinated in a blend of herbs and spices. The meat is cooked uniformly and kept soft and juicy because of the gradual rotation of the rotisserie. Once the meat has finished cooking, it is thinly sliced and placed in a warm pita with tomato, onion, and tzatziki sauce. Tzatziki sauce gives a meal a deliciously tangy taste and is a creamy, garlicky sauce prepared with yogurt, cucumber, garlic, and olive oil.

Gyro's adaptability is one of its best qualities. Depending on the individual's desire, there are several methods to serve it. Some enjoy their gyros with a side of Greek salad or roasted potatoes, while others prefer theirs with fries or grilled veggies within the pita bread. The meat and toppings of the gyro may also be placed on a bed of rice or fries when it's served on a platter.

Gyro vendors and restaurants may be found all around the city of Athens. In Athens, some of the most well-known gyro eateries include Bairaktaris, O Kostas, and Thanasis. These eateries have been providing the city with delectable gyros for decades and have established themselves as landmarks.

Gourmet gyros have been more popular in recent years as chefs experiment with various meats and garnishes to produce novel and intriguing tastes. For instance, some eateries provide gyros made from duck, beef, or even octopus, while others season the meat with various sauces or spices to produce interesting and delectable meals.

The Greek cuisine gyro has gained popularity as a satisfying and delectable street meal all around the globe. It is the ideal fast and simple supper since it is made with marinated meat that is roasted on a vertical rotisserie and served on warm pita bread with tomato, onion, and tzatziki sauce. Gyros are a must-try while visiting Athens, whether you want them with fries, salad, or simply the traditional toppings.

Ouzo: Similar to sambuca or arak, this traditional Greek liqueur is created from anise. It is a traditional aperitif that is a must-try for everyone who wishes to experience Greek culture. It is often served with a small dish of meze.

Traditional Greek liqueur ouzo has long been a favorite of both residents and visitors. Anise is a blooming plant that is indigenous to the southwest Asian and eastern Mediterranean regions and is used to make this alcoholic beverage. The liquor has a distinct taste and scent that are often contrasted with other anise-based liquors like sambuca and arak.

As an aperitif, or a beverage drunk before a meal to pique appetite, ouzo is often offered. It is often served with a small plate of meze, which is a variety of tiny meals that are given as appetizers. It is typically served in a small glass with a few ice cubes. Locals often choose ouzo and meze together since it's a delicious way to sample Greek cuisine.

Making ouzo is a difficult procedure that calls for knowledge and expertise. Water, anise, and other botanicals including coriander, fennel, and mastic are combined to create the spirit. The mixture of the components is distilled to produce a clear liquid that is then packaged and sold.

The fact that ouzo becomes hazy when water is added is one of its most distinctive characteristics. Due to the anise oil in the spirit's inability to dissolve in water, the drink takes on a milky white hue as a result. One of the characteristics of ouzo that makes it so distinctive is what is known as the ouzo effect.

People of various ages and backgrounds appreciate ouzo, and it's a common beverage for gathering with friends and celebrating. In fact, it's often called the national beverage of Greece, and many Greeks take pleasure in it.

If you're in Athens, you may sample ouzo at a variety of establishments, including quaint tavernas, taverns, and eateries. Plomari, Mini, and Barbayanni are among the most well-known ouzo brands, and each has a distinctive taste and scent. Ouzo may be consumed alone or combined with water or other drinks like soda or juice.

In general, ouzo is a crucial component of Greek culture and is something that everyone visiting Athens should sample. Ouzo is a fantastic option if you like anise-flavored alcoholic beverages or are simply seeking to try something different. So why not raise a glass and toast this delectable and distinctive Greek spirit with "yamas"?

Metaxa: This Greek brandy is produced from grape spirits and wine and is aged in wood barrels. It's a well-liked after-dinner beverage and is available at many taverns and eateries in Athens.

Produced from a combination of wine and grape spirits that have been distilled, and it is then aged in oak barrels to give it a unique taste character. In Greece, Metaxa is a preferred digestif and a common after-dinner beverage.

Spyros Metaxa produced the first batch of this unusual spirit in 1888, which is when it originally became known as Metaxa.

Originally, Metaxa was intended to be a smoother, more sophisticated alternative to the traditional Greek brandy, which was renowned for its acrid and flaming flavor. For a more well-rounded and harmonious taste, Spyros Metaxa combined wines and grape spirits from different parts of Greece.

The same conventional techniques that were used more than a century ago are being utilized to make Metaxa today. The meticulously crafted combination of wine and grape spirits is then stored in oak barrels for a minimum of three years, giving the spirit its distinct taste and silky finish.

The length of time that Metaxa has spent maturing in oak barrels determines its classification. The newest Metaxa, dubbed Metaxa Three Star, is at least three years old and boasts a smooth, fruity taste with hints of vanilla and honey. With flavors of oak, spice, and dried fruit, Metaxa Five Star, which has been matured for a minimum of five years, has a more nuanced taste profile. The most expensive kind of Metaxa, Metaxa Seven Star, has been matured for a minimum of seven years and has a rich, strong taste with hints of dark chocolate and coffee.

Metaxa may be sipped alone, used as a foundation for cocktails, or consumed as a standalone beverage. As a method to unwind and relax after a meal, it is often provided after supper. Desserts, especially sweet pastries, and chocolate go well with it.

In addition to several pubs and eateries, liquor shops, and supermarkets, Metaxa is available throughout Athens. According to the customer's taste, it is often served either chilled or at room temperature. The fact that Metaxa is a well-liked gift item for tourists to take home makes it a favorite among Athenians as well.

Overall, both residents and tourists alike adore the distinctive and excellent Greek brandy known as Metaxa. Because of its smoothness and complexity of taste, it is a favorite ingredient for cocktails and a superb after-dinner beverage. Try Metaxa if you're in Athens to enjoy the many tastes and customs of Greek culture.

Frappé: The ingredients for this Greek iced coffee are instant coffee, water, and sugar, and it is served over ice. It is a cool, invigorating beverage that is ideal for a hot day.

Greek iced coffee known as frappé has become a symbol of Greek culture. It is a cool, invigorating beverage that is great on hot days or whenever you need a pick-me-up. On ice, frappé is created using instant coffee, water, and sugar.

The first frappé was served in the 1950s at the International Trade Fair in Thessaloniki by a Nescafé salesperson by the name of Dimitris Vakondios, who was introducing the brand's new instant coffee at the time. Vakondios decided to make a frothy foam by combining the instant coffee with cold water, ice, and shaking it briskly since he was out of hot water for his coffee. The outcome was a smashing success, and frappé spread like wildfire across Greece.

Nowadays, frappé is a mainstay of Greek coffee culture and is available practically everywhere in the nation's cafes and eateries. It may be created with various kinds of sugar and milk to suit your preferences and is normally served in a tall glass with a straw. Although some people like their frappés sweet, some do not, and others like to add a splash of milk or cream for a fuller taste, it depends on the individual.

You'll need ice, water, sugar, and instant coffee to create frappé. Then, combine 1 teaspoon of instant coffee with 1 teaspoon of sugar, or more, to taste. After the water has been added, shake or combine the mixture quickly until it froths and turns creamy. After that, add ice to a large glass and pour the coffee mixture over it. Next, fill the glass with water and thoroughly swirl. You may now enjoy your frappé!

Particularly on a hot day, frappé is a terrific alternative for a reviving and revitalizing beverage. Frappés are also a well-liked social beverage, and you'll often find families and groups of friends conversing and drinking them together in outdoor cafés. Frappé is a flexible beverage that can be savored at any time of day and is a wonderful way to experience Greece's easygoing and welcoming culture.

Outside of Greece, frappé has grown in popularity recently and is now available in many other nations' cafés and eateries. Yet, Greece continues to be the country with which it is most closely linked, and it is an adored and enduring aspect of Greek coffee culture.

Baklava: Using layers of phyllo dough, honey, and chopped nuts—usually walnuts or pistachios—this dessert is prepared. Anybody with a sweet taste will love this scrumptious treat.

Popular in Greece and the Middle East, baklava is a sweet pastry. With layers of phyllo dough, honey, and chopped nuts—usually walnuts or pistachios—it is a delectable treat. The pastry, which is a favorite delicacy for special occasions, is often sliced into little diamond-shaped pieces.

There is substantial disagreement over the history of baklava. Some historians think it came from the Byzantine Empire, while others think the Turks introduced it to the area. Regardless of where it came from, baklava has spread around the globe and has become a symbol of the Mediterranean.

The distinctive texture of baklava is one of its many exceptional qualities. The phyllo dough layers are thin and crispy, and the honey and almonds provide a sticky, chewy feel that is wonderfully gratifying. Baklava is an utterly enticing delicacy due to the blend of tastes and textures.

Baklava-making is a time-consuming procedure that demands a lot of patience and talent. It is necessary to lay out the phyllo dough very thinly before brushing it with melted butter or oil. A combination of honey and almonds is then placed between each layer as the layers are layered on top of one another. After the dough has been assembled completely, it is cooked in the oven until it is crisp and golden brown.

Baklava comes in a wide variety, and every location has its own distinctive way of preparing it. To give the pastry a flowery and aromatic scent, some recipes ask for rose water or orange blossom water to be added to the honey mixture. Some add their own unique taste by using other nuts, including almonds or pecans.

The use of premium ingredients is one aspect that unites all baklava recipes. To make a dessert that is genuinely wonderful, the phyllo dough must be fresh and the nuts must be of the best caliber. Another crucial component is honey, which many bakers choose to include since it gives the pastry a distinctive taste and depth.

Baklava is a delicious delicacy that is ideal for special events like weddings, festivals, and religious festivities. It is often served with coffee or tea. It is also a fantastic choice for individuals who like sweets and want to treat themselves to a luxurious treat.

Baklava is a specialty dish that is widely available in bakeries and sweet stores across Athens and is a must-try for tourists. There is a baklava for everyone, whether you favor the conventional walnut filling or wish to try a more unique variant. So while visiting Athens, make sure to include this delectable dessert on your list of delicacies to taste.

A vacation to Athens would not be complete without sampling some of the city's other delectable dishes and beverages.

Shopping in Athens

Athens is a terrific place to go shopping since it provides both residents and visitors with a variety of possibilities. Everyone can find something they like, whether they want designer clothing or authentic Greek trinkets. Some of the top places to shop in Athens are listed below:

Ermou Street: This is Athens' largest shopping street, and it is dotted with a variety of stores, from well-known worldwide chains to independent boutiques. The pedestrianized street is a fantastic location for a leisurely retail walk.

One of the most well-liked shopping areas in Athens is Ermou Street, which has a wide selection of shops and goods to suit everyone's demands. The street, which runs from Syntagma Square to Monastiraki and is in the center of the city, is readily accessible from most areas of Athens. The roadway is pedestrianized, making it a wonderful location for a leisurely walk while shopping.

A broad variety of shops line Ermou Street, from local boutiques selling one-of-a-kind items to worldwide chains like H&M, Zara, and Mango. High-end fashion as well as reasonably priced apparel, shoes, and accessories are also available to shoppers. Many department shops, notably the well-known Greek cosmetics and beauty retailer Hondos Center, are also located on Ermou Street.

Ermou Street has a large selection of shops that sell presents and souvenirs, including regional specialties, handcrafted items, and traditional Greek goods, in addition to apparel and accessories. Also, there are several cafés, eateries, and street sellers that provide food and beverages for customers to enjoy as they shop.

The ambiance and vibe of Ermou Street itself are among the best parts of shopping there. A bright and energetic environment is created by the pedestrianized area's constant throng of consumers and street entertainers. The beautiful architecture and old buildings that line the street are enjoyed by shoppers, adding to the allure of the shopping experience.

Ermou Street has several events and festivals all year long, adding to its allure as a place for shopping. A spectacular shopping experience is created during the holiday season when the street is converted into a winter wonderland with colorful lights and decorations. Fashion displays, musical performances, and cultural festivals are additional events.

Anybody visiting Athens should make sure to go shopping on Ermou Street. It provides a distinctive and memorable shopping experience with a large variety of shops and goods, a buzzing environment, and a convenient location. Ermou Street offers a wide range of goods, from designer clothing to authentic Greek trinkets.

Monastiraki Flea Market: The lively market in the center of Athens is a terrific spot to purchase handcrafted goods and unusual gifts. Everything is available, from antique clothes to jewelry and pottery made traditionally in Greece.

At the base of the Acropolis in Athens' Monastiraki neighborhood, a bustling market called the Monastiraki Flea Market can be found. Both residents and visitors should make time to visit one of Athens's most well-known and historic marketplaces.

The market is a labyrinth of little stores, kiosks, and vendors offering a wide variety of goods, from vintage apparel and antique furniture to handcrafted jewelry and traditional Greek ceramics. You may pick up a one-of-a-kind souvenir from Athens here to take with you.

The antique sector of the Monastiraki Flea Market is one of its attractions. Vintage posters, old pictures, furniture, and different household goods are just a few of the unusual products available at antique stores. Here is the ideal location for both searching for unique gems and just perusing the variety of curiosities and curios.

The market is also an excellent location to get authentically Greek trinkets like leather sandals, woven linens, and handcrafted pottery. Greek goods including olive oil, honey, and traditional sweets are available in a wide variety of stores and booths.

The Monastiraki Flea Market is a busy location with a vibrant atmosphere, and it's worthwhile to spend some time exploring the little lanes to find all the treasures that are concealed away.

There are several quaint tavernas, cafés, and taverns in the neighborhood for those who wish to unwind after shopping. A lively and thrilling mood is often created by music and the aroma of freshly cooked cuisine filling the streets.

The Monastiraki Flea Market is an exceptional place to shop and really reflects the spirit of Athens. It's a terrific spot to spend a few hours perusing, taking in the bustling ambiance of the market, and hunting out some interesting mementos to bring home.

Kolonaki: Some of the most upmarket shops and designer businesses in the city may be found in this affluent area. This is the location to go if you're seeking high-end clothing and accessories.

In the heart of Athens, at the foot of Lycabettus Hill, sits the chic area of Kolonaki. It is popular with the city's fashion-conscious audience because of its high-end shops, designer stores, and upmarket eateries.

A wide variety of local and international designer retailers, including Chanel, Prada, Gucci, Louis Vuitton, and Dior, are available in Kolonaki. The majority of the designer boutiques are found along Voukourestiou Street, where you can shop for the newest styles in high-end clothing, accessories, shoes, and jewelry. There are a number of smaller, independent boutiques that sell distinctive, one-of-a-kind items in addition to the high-end shops.

Kolonaki is a fantastic place for art enthusiasts in addition to being a hotspot for fashion. There are several galleries in the neighborhood that display the creations of both well-known and emerging artists. The Skoufa Gallery, which features works by modern Greek and foreign artists, is among the most well-known.

Kolonaki also has a ton of hip cafés and eateries if you need a break from shopping. The local culinary scene is vibrant, offering everything from classic Greek tavernas to contemporary fusion dishes. Some of the favorites among coffee connoisseurs are well-known coffee shops like Mokka, Taf Coffee, and Coffee Island.

The scenic alleys of Kolonaki are ideal for wandering around and taking in the neighborhood's energetic vibe. When exploring the region, you may discover numerous hidden treasures, including tiny boutique stores, street art, and classic Greek buildings. The

Lycabettus Hill, which provides breathtaking panoramic views of the city and the Acropolis, is one of the must-see locations in Kolonaki.

For those interested in splurging on upscale clothing, great art, and good cuisine in Athens, Kolonaki is a must-visit location. It provides a fun eating and shopping experience in a pleasant and posh area.

Plaka: The classic Greek buildings and winding lanes of this lovely area are well-known. Together with authentic Greek cuisine and beverages, it is a terrific spot to discover souvenirs and handmade items.

In the center of Athens, near the Acropolis, lies the lovely district known as Plaka. It is one of the oldest districts in the city, and both visitors and residents like it for its distinctive character created by its small streets and classic Greek buildings.

With a wide range of shops selling anything from high-end clothing and jewelry to souvenirs and handicrafts, Plaka is renowned for its fantastic shopping possibilities. Adrianou Street, which is packed with stores offering traditional Greek mementos including ceramics, pottery, and textiles, is one of Plaka's busiest shopping avenues. The costs are often relatively affordable, making this an excellent spot to discover unusual presents to send home.

Plaka is an excellent spot to obtain authentic Greek meals and beverages in addition to souvenirs. There are several tavernas and restaurants serving delectable Greek food, as well as pubs and cafés where you may unwind and take in a coffee or other beverage. The picturesque Anafiotika district in Plaka, where you can discover little eateries and pubs buried away in winding lanes, is one of the most well-liked spots for food and beverages.

There are several possibilities in Plaka if you're seeking designer clothing and jewelry. Several expensive shops and jewelry stores can be found in the area, selling anything from designer apparel to fine jewelry. Karyatis, a store that specialized in traditional Greek apparel and accessories, is among the most well-known stores in Plaka.

The Monastiraki Flea Market is another well-liked shopping location in Plaka and is just a short walk away. Vintage clothes, antiques, and other interesting stuff may be found in plenty at this crowded market. Except on Sundays, the market is open every day, and the prices are often extremely reasonable.

In general, Plaka is a fantastic location for consumers of all tastes and price ranges. You will undoubtedly find something that strikes your attention in this attractive area, whether you're shopping for high-end clothing, distinctive antique items, or traditional Greek souvenirs. Moreover, Plaka is a terrific spot to unwind and take in the local culture while you shop thanks to its abundance of cafés, pubs, and restaurants.

Attica: One of Athens' biggest and busiest shopping areas is this department store. It provides a broad variety of items, including electronics, home goods, clothing, and cosmetic products.

At the center of the city's business core lies the well-known department store Attica. It is one of Athens' biggest and most well-known shopping areas, providing a variety of goods from renowned worldwide companies as well as regional designers. Attica is a must-visit spot for every serious shopper because of its superb location and wide range.

Fashion enthusiasts will appreciate Attica's wide assortment of apparel, accessories, and shoes. Many of the most well-known international labels, including Gucci, Prada, and Balenciaga, as well as regional designers like Christos Costarellos and Sophia Kokosalaki, are represented in the shop. Attica is a fantastic choice for customers with different budgets since it provides a broad variety of pricing ranges, from inexpensive essentials to high-end luxury products.

A large range of skincare, cosmetics, and fragrance items from both domestic and foreign brands are available at Attica in addition to clothing. Popular brands like Chanel, Dior, and Estée Lauder are featured in the store's beauty area, along with regional ones like Apivita and Korres. The skilled team can provide professional guidance on the appropriate products for your skin type and issues.

Attica provides a variety of high-quality home items, including furniture, bedding, and home décor, for individuals wishing to freshen up their homes. The shop offers a variety of goods from both foreign and regional manufacturers, such as Fornasetti, Jonathan Adler, and Hellenic Home. For anybody wishing to update their home décor, Attica is a terrific choice because of its wide assortment of fashionable and useful goods.

For foodies, Attica is a terrific vacation spot. Olive oil, honey, and wine are among the premium, regionally produced goods available in the store's gourmet cuisine department. The shop also has a food hall with a number of eateries and cafés that serve a variety of international cuisines. Attica's culinary hall provides something for everyone, from sushi to Greek meze.

For anybody interested in fashion, cosmetics, home products, or fine dining, Attica is a must-visit location. Attica is one of the greatest places to shop in Athens because of its excellent location, wide range of goods, and experienced employees.

The Mall Athens: This contemporary retail area, which is situated close to the city, has both Greek and foreign brands. Together with restaurants and other leisure opportunities, it offers a movie theater.

A contemporary retail complex called The Mall Athens lies close to the city's core in the northeastern suburb of Marousi. With a variety of food, entertainment, and retail opportunities, it is a well-liked tourist and local attraction.

Almost 200 shops, including both foreign and Greek brands, can be found in the mall. Everything from designer clothing to daily necessities, as well as gadgets, books, and home items, are available for shoppers. Among the most well-known retailers are Zara, H&M, Mango, and Sephora.

The Mall Athens has a range of eating alternatives, including sit-down restaurants and fast food. Greek delicacies, foreign cuisine, and even a food court with a variety of selections are available to visitors. The mall also has a movie theater complex with a number of cinemas showcasing the most recent releases.

The Mall Athens offers a range of entertainment-related events all year long, like concerts, fashion displays, and cultural exhibits. For information on events taking place while they are there, visitors may check the mall's website.

The architecture and design of The Mall Athens is one of its distinctive qualities. The mall was constructed in an open-air, contemporary design with tall ceilings and plenty of natural light. For shoppers and tourists, the design integrates natural areas and water elements to create a warm and comfortable ambiance.

There are a few additional places of interest close to The Mall Athens that people could check out if they want to take a break from shopping. Both the Athens Olympic Sports Complex and the Olympic Stadium, which hosted the 2004 Summer Olympics, are close by. During the year, a number of exhibits and events are also held at the neighboring Helexpo Palace.

If you're searching for a contemporary shopping experience in Athens, go to The Mall Athens. It has something for everyone in terms of retail, food, and entertainment, and its distinctive architecture and design elevate it to the status of a desirable travel destination in and of itself.

Athens Central Market: Fresh fruit, meat, and seafood, as well as spices and other culinary items, may all be found at this crowded market. It's a fantastic location to sample the local food and buy Greek cooking supplies.

Every gourmet visiting Athens must go to the Athens Central Market, usually referred to as the Varvakios Agora. This market, which is located in the center of the city, is a hive of activity, with sellers offering a broad range of fresh food items. You can find everything here to suit your preferences, whether you're shopping for fish, meat, veggies, or spices.

From its founding in the late 19th century, the market has played a significant role in Athenian culture. It's a well-liked tourist site nowadays and a fantastic spot to sample regional food. The chance to speak with the sellers, who are often enthusiastic about their goods and eager to impart their expertise to customers, is one of the nicest aspects of the market.

When you go around the market, you'll discover a huge selection of fresh seafood, including sardines, octopus, and more. A vast range of meats, including lamb, hog, and beef, as well as offal like liver and intestines, are also available. Also, there is a great range of locally produced products available, including tomatoes, cucumbers, eggplants, and other vegetables and fruits.

The market is a fantastic location to buy spices, dried fruits, nuts, and other food items in addition to fresh food items. Vendors may be seen selling dried figs, apricots, and other fruits and vegetables, as well as anything from saffron to paprika to cinnamon. You may sample products from many of the sellers before you purchase them.

Beyond the culinary items, the market is a fantastic location to get a sense of Athens' culture. A sight to witness is the market's commotion, as sellers yell out their items and shoppers haggle for the best deals. The market is a terrific area to people-watch as well since it attracts folks from all walks of life who are out buying and mingling.

For everyone interested in cuisine and culture, a trip to the Athens Central Market is a must. It's a terrific spot to enjoy the bright atmosphere of Athens, sample the local food, and talk to merchants. The market is a must-stop on any trip to Athens, whether you're looking for supplies to prepare your own Greek food or just want to take it all in.

Overall, Athens is a fantastic shopping destination, with a vast selection of products for every taste and price range. You're likely to discover something you adore, whether you're seeking designer clothing or vintage Greek mementos.

Chapter 4: Day Trips from Athens

Delphi

Delphi: Around 120 kilometers (km) northwest of Athens, Delphi is a significant archaeological site that was once thought to be the geographic center of the globe. The Theatre of Delphi, the Sanctuary of Athena Pronaia, and the Temple of Apollo's remains may all be found here. Delphi itself is a lovely village with winding lanes and authentic Greek tavernas.

Delphi is an essential stop on any day trip from Athens. On the western side of Mount Parnassus, with a view of the Gulf of Corinth, is where the ancient city of Delphi may be found. The famed

Apollon oracle was located there, and it was regarded as the center of the universe in ancient Greece. The location is now a significant archaeological and historical destination as well as a UNESCO World Heritage Site.

The Temple of Apollo, which was constructed in the 4th century BC, is Delphi's principal draw. The famed Delphi oracle, which the ancient Greeks sought for insight from the gods, had its home in the temple. The priests and priestesses of the temple deciphered the oracle's complex and sometimes ambiguous utterances. Visitors to the location may examine the temple's remains and discover more about the oracle's significance in ancient Greece.

The Sanctuary of Athena Pronaia is another significant landmark in Delphi. The goddess Athena was honored at this temple, which stood at the base of Mount Parnassus. The sanctuary is home to a number of significant structures, including the Gymnasium where young men trained for athletic contests, and the Tholos, a circular structure with a particular architectural style.

A visit to the Theatre of Delphi is highly recommended. The theater, which was constructed in the 4th century BC and had 5,000 seats, was used for both theatrical plays and religious rituals. The theatre's remains may be explored by visitors who can then envision what it must have been like to see a play or ceremony there.

Together with the historic attractions, Delphi itself is a delightful town that is well worth a visit. The village, which is perched on Mount Parnassus's flanks, is dotted with winding lanes, classic Greek tavernas, and boutiques offering regional handicrafts and trinkets. When strolling around the village, visitors may take in the stunning views of the mountains and surrounding landscape.

Visitors have two transportation options from Athens to Delphi: bus or car. By vehicle, it takes around 2.5 hours, while by bus it takes about 3 hours. There are several picturesque stops along the route as the road meanders through stunning landscapes and mountains. Another option for visitors is to reserve a guided trip to Delphi, which includes transportation from Athens, a tour guide, and access to the historic location.

Delphi is a wonderful day excursion from Athens that allows tourists to see both the lovely village of Delphi and the rich history and culture of ancient Greece. Delphi is a must-see location in Greece whether you're interested in history, or archaeology, or simply want to see a stunning location.

Aegina Island

Aegina Island: Aegina is a little island that is only accessible by boat from Athens. It is renowned for its stunning beaches, pure seas, and lovely town, which has neoclassical architecture and winding lanes. The world's greatest pistachios may be found on the island; be sure to sample them.

With just a short boat journey from Athens, Aegina Island is a well-liked day vacation location. From picturesque beaches and pristine oceans to quaint villages and historical landmarks, this little island has a lot to offer. The best attractions on Aegina Island are listed below.

The beaches of Aegina are one of its key attractions. Agia Marina, a long sandy beach on the island's north coast, and Perdika, a charming fishing hamlet with a little beach and clean seas, are only two of the island's stunning beaches. Visit Marathonas Beach on the island's east coast for a more private experience. Here, you may swim and sunbathe in a serene, natural environment.

Together with its neoclassical architecture, winding lanes, and ancient tavernas, Aegina is renowned for its lovely town. The harbor, where fishing boats and yachts are moored side by side, is the focal point of the town. The town is a terrific area to roam about and take in the sights and sounds of the island because of its vibrant and welcoming vibe.

The Temple of Aphaia, an ancient Greek temple devoted to the goddess Aphaia, is one of the primary attractions of Aegina. The temple provides breathtaking views of the surrounding area from its hilltop location overlooking the sea. One of the finest preserved ancient Greek temples in the world, the temple dates to the 5th century BC. Be sure to join a guided tour of the temple to discover its importance and history.

The Monastery of Saint Nectarios, a stunning monastery in Byzantine architecture that is one of the most significant pilgrimage destinations in Greece, is another must-see sight on Aegina. The early 20th-century monastery was constructed in honor of Saint Nectarios, a living saint renowned for his miracles and healing abilities. The monastery contains a lovely courtyard and a modest museum where you can find out more about Saint Nectarios' life and activities.

Aegina's famed pistachios must also be sampled to make a trip there complete. One of the world's biggest pistachio growers, Aegina is renowned for the superior flavor and quality of its pistachios. They are available at neighborhood stores and markets, and many taverns and restaurants include them in their menus.

Beautiful beaches, quaint villages, historical attractions, and delectable cuisine can all be found on the island of Aegina, a perfect day trip from Athens. Everyone can find something to do on the island of Aegina, whether they want to relax on the beach, see historic Greek temples, or sample the local delicacy, pistachios.

Corinth Canal

The Saronic Gulf and the Gulf of Corinth are connected by a man-made canal known as the Corinth Canal. It is roughly 80 kilometers west of Athens and is a fantastic site to visit because of its amazing engineering and breathtaking scenery.

The Saronic Gulf and the Gulf of Corinth are connected by a small body of water known as the Corinth Canal. Ships passing between the Ionian and Aegean Seas may use it as a shortcut since it divides the Peloponnese peninsula from the Greek mainland. The canal, which was constructed in the late 19th century, is a remarkable technical achievement.

Ancient civilizations had the notion of building a canal across the Isthmus of Corinth. While they gave it some thought, the ancient Greeks ultimately decided against it because of the complexity and expense of the undertaking. The concept wasn't brought up again until the nineteenth century. A French corporation started building the canal in 1881, but the endeavor was fraught with challenges, including budgetary issues and landslides. It took more than ten years to complete the project, which was finally finished in 1893.

The canal is about 6.4 kilometers long, 23 meters broad, and has cliffs that may become as high as 80 meters. It is a magnificent site to see and a well-liked destination for tourists coming to Greece. Taking a boat excursion is one of the greatest ways to enjoy the canal. There are several companies that provide quick tours of the canal that last for approximately an hour. The canal's narrowness and the tall walls on each side may be seen up close on these cruises, allowing you to fully appreciate them.

With several routes that provide breathtaking views of the canal and the surrounding area, the Corinth Canal is also a fantastic location for trekking. Throughout the canal, there are several observation sites that provide excellent picture ops. It's a wonderful location to spend a day seeing Greece's natural beauty and discovering its extensive history.

There are several more attractions in the vicinity in addition to the canal itself. A number of historical landmarks, including the remains of the Temple of Apollo and the old Roman settlement of Lechaion, are found close by in the ancient city of Corinth. Moreover, the city is home to a museum with exhibits tracing the history of the area from prehistoric times to the present.

The Acrocorinth, a stronghold perched on a mountain overlooking the city of Corinth, is another close sight. The old fortification gives breathtaking views of the surrounding area and has a long and intriguing history.

Each visitor to Greece must make time to see the Corinth Canal. The canal has much to offer whether you're interested in engineering, history, or the beauty of nature. It's a wonderful destination to spend a day exploring and learning about the rich culture and history of Greece because of its breathtaking vistas, hiking paths, and close-by historical landmarks.

Cape Sounion

Cape Sounion: The Temple of Poseidon, a historic Greek temple with breathtaking views of the Aegean Sea, is found on Cape Sounion, which is about 70 kilometers southeast of Athens. One of the finest preserved ancient Greek temples in the world, the temple dates to the 5th century BC.

For good reason, Cape Sounion is a popular day excursion from Athens. Cape Sounion, which is situated on the southernmost point of the Attic Peninsula, provides breathtaking views of the Aegean Sea and the nearby shoreline. The Temple of Poseidon, an illustrious and mythical ancient Greek temple, is also located there.

One of the finest preserved ancient Greek temples in the world is the Temple of Poseidon, which dates to the 5th century BC. It was part of a larger complex of structures that included comprised a sanctuary, a fortification wall, and numerous smaller temples. It was built in honor of Poseidon, the deity of the sea. It is said that the sea deity himself picked the site of the temple, which is perched on a rocky peninsula with a view of the ocean.

Nowadays, tourists are welcome to explore the temple remains and enjoy the stunning Aegean Sea views. 16 six-meter-tall Doric columns may be seen in the marble temple. The temple still exists as a monument to the engineering and design of ancient Greece, despite the devastation done by earthquakes and other natural calamities throughout the years.

Capc Sounion is home to a number of other fascinating locations in addition to the Temple of Poseidon. The surrounding town of Sounio, with its quaint alleys, little cafés, and lovely port, provides a peek into traditional Greek life. Also, visitors have the option of taking a boat tour of the local islands or just unwinding on one of the numerous nearby beaches.

Watching the sunset from the temple is one of the most well-liked things to do in Cape Sounion. The temple glows golden as the sun sets over the Aegean Sea, and the vistas are unmatched. A modest café serving food and drinks is next to the temple, giving it the ideal spot to relax and take in the scenery.

From Athens, Cape Sounion is not difficult to reach. Together with private excursions and taxis, various bus trips leave from the city's center. The trip takes approximately an hour and a half, and the route follows a beautiful coastal road with breathtaking views of the surrounding area and the water.

See one of the best-preserved ancient Greek temples in the world and take in the natural beauty of Greece on a day excursion to Cape Sounion. Cape Sounion is unquestionably worthwhile a visit, whether you're a history enthusiast, a wildlife enthusiast, or just searching for a tranquil day excursion from Athens.

Mycenae

Mycenae, which lies roughly 120 kilometers southwest of Athens, was one of the principal centers of ancient Greek civilization. Explore the ancient city's remains here, which include the well-known Lion Gate, the Tomb of Agamemnon, and the Palace of Mycenae.

A fascinating archaeological site, Mycenae provides tourists with a window into the vibrant past and culture of ancient Greece. Mycenae, one of the most significant towns of the Mycenaean civilization, was situated in the northern Peloponnese area and had a significant impact on the formation of ancient Greek culture.

The well-known Lion Gate, which serves as the city's main entrance, is among Mycenae's most striking characteristics. This enormous stone gate, which dates to the 13th century BC, is adorned with two lion statues. Anybody visiting the location must view the Lion Gate, which is regarded as one of the most spectacular specimens of Mycenaean construction.

The Tomb of Agamemnon, which is said to be the last resting place of the mythical ruler of Mycenae, is another significant site in Mycenae. The tomb is a massive stone building with a beehive form that is carved with fine details. Visitors may see the burial chamber within the tomb and marvel at the impressive engineering that went into its creation.

Another significant location in the ancient city is the Palace of Mycenae. The royal family and their entourage are thought to have resided in this vast collection of structures, which served as the hub of social and political activity in Mycenae. Visitors may still tour the remains of the Great Hall, the Throne Room, and other significant palace structures, despite the fact that most of the complex is now in ruins.

Visitors to Mycenae may also tour the ancient city's walls, which are among the oldest and most spectacular in Greece in addition to these significant sites. The walls, which were created to keep out attackers, are made of large stone blocks. An excellent approach to understanding the size and significance of the old city is to stroll around the city walls.

Mycenae is surrounded by breathtaking natural beauty, including rolling hills, olive orchards, and vineyards, in addition to the ancient monuments. Take a stroll across the nearby countryside to experience a tranquil, rural setting that is a world apart from the bustle and noise of contemporary Athens.

Visitors have two transportation options from Athens to Mycenae: buses or rented cars. The trip takes around two hours, but it is worth taking because of the beautiful landscape along the route. There are several guided excursions that may provide a thorough examination of Mycenae's history and culture as well.

Everyone interested in the history and culture of the ancient Greeks should make a trip to Mycenae. It is an interesting and worthwhile day excursion from Athens because of its spectacular ruins, breathtaking natural beauty, and rich history.

Hydra Island

A quick boat trip from Athens will take you to the tiny, car-free island of Hydra. It is renowned for its picturesque town with its winding lanes and classic Greek architecture, as well as its stunning beaches and pristine seas. It's a wonderful location to decompress and unwind for the day.

A popular day excursion from Athens is to Hydra Island because of its stunning landscape, laid-back vibe, and interesting history. The island sits in the Aegean Sea, and travelers may take a ferry there from the port of Piraeus, which is close to Athens.

Visitors are instantly charmed by the island upon arrival. Visitors may amble around Hydra's main town's winding alleys and alleyways without having to contend with traffic noise or exhaust pollution. The town's whitewashed houses and vibrant shutters are typical of traditional Greek architecture. Tourists may peruse specialty stores, art galleries, and local artisan markets, or they can just unwind at a café and take in the relaxed ambiance.

The stunning beaches and pristine seas of Hydra are among its key attractions. Swimming, tanning, and a variety of water sports, such as kayaking and snorkeling, are all available to visitors. Vlychos, Bisti, and Avlaki are among the island's busiest beaches. A boat tour of the island is another option for those who want to explore some of the more remote coves and beaches.

In addition to its stunning natural surroundings, Hydra has a lengthy past. The island was a significant hub for trade and commerce in the Mediterranean and played a significant part in the early 19th-century Greek War of Independence. The Historical Archives Museum of Hydra, which keeps a collection of records and relics connected to the island's past, offers visitors further information about the history of the island.

The Monastery of the Assumption of the Virgin Mary, which is perched on a hill overlooking the town of Hydra, is another well-liked tourist destination. The monastery, which was founded in the 17th century, has a stunning church with a large iconostasis as well as a museum that houses a variety of religious artifacts.

Drinks and food play a significant role in the Hydra experience. The island is well-known for its fresh seafood, and tourists may sample a variety of mouthwatering delicacies in neighborhood tavernas and eateries. Octopus on the grill, fish roe, and shrimp saganaki are some of the dishes that are most well-liked. Also, visitors may try regional wines, including the sweet dessert wine known as "mastiha," which is produced from a native tree's resin.

A day trip to Hydra Island is a wonderful way to take in Greece's natural beauty and authentic charm. Hydra has plenty to offer everyone, whether you want to relax on the beach, take in some culture or history, or all three. It's an easy and convenient destination for a day trip or a longer stay given its proximity to Athens.

Chapter 5: Museums and Cultural Attractions in Athens

The Acropolis Museum

In Athens, Greece, there is a top-notch museum called the Acropolis Museum. It was made accessible to the public in 2009 and is devoted to the Athens Acropolis's archaeological discoveries. Every visitor interested in Greek history and culture should pay a visit to the museum.

Thousands of ancient artifacts, including pottery, sculptures, and other items discovered during Acropolis site excavations, may be seen at the Acropolis Museum. The museum is organized into numerous parts, each of which is devoted to a certain era in the

Acropolis' history. The Parthenon Gallery, which displays the sculptures from the Parthenon temple, is the most well-known area of the museum.

One of the most magnificent sections of the museum is the Parthenon Gallery, which is devoted to the Parthenon temple, one of the most significant structures on the Acropolis. Many authentic sculptures and friezes that were taken from the Parthenon temple during the 19th century may be found in the gallery, which was built to mimic the Parthenon temple's size. The frieze that runs along the top of the inner walls of the gallery and shows events from the Panathenaic procession, a significant celebration in ancient Athens, is the most well-known of these sculptures.

The Acropolis Museum features a number of additional parts in addition to the Parthenon Gallery, each of which is devoted to a distinct period in the history of the Acropolis. For instance, the Archaic Gallery honors the ancient era and displays a variety of sculptures and other items that were discovered on the Acropolis site. Many sizable sculptures that once graced the Propylaea, the imposing doorway to the Acropolis, are housed in the Propylaea Gallery, which is devoted to it.

The museum also hosts a variety of transient exhibits that switch up from time to time. These exhibits provide visitors the chance to learn more about certain facets of the ancient world and cover a broad variety of themes relating to Greek history and culture.

The design of the Acropolis Museum is among its most distinctive aspects. The museum, which was erected on the site of a historic settlement, was intended to blend in with the nearby archaeological site. Visitors may see the excavations of the historic neighborhood below thanks to the museum's glass ground floor. The museum is a wonderful spot to relax and appreciate the beauty of the neighborhood since it also offers a large outdoor patio with views of the Acropolis.

The many conveniences offered by the Acropolis Museum are also available to visitors. There is a bookstore where visitors may buy books about Greek history and culture in addition to a café and gift shop within the museum. Also, the museum provides visitors with guided tours that provide them with an in-depth understanding of the treasures and the Acropolis' history.

Anybody interested in Greek history and culture must visit the Acropolis Museum. It provides guests with a unique experience because of its remarkable collections, distinctive design, and top-notch facilities. The Acropolis Museum is a must-see for anybody interested in history, art, or simply finding a fantastic location to unwind and learn more about ancient civilization.

The National Archaeological Museum

One of Greece's biggest and most significant museums, as well as one of the most significant archaeological museums in the whole world, is the National Archaeological Museum of Athens. It was established in the late 19th century to store and exhibit the various ancient antiques and riches uncovered in Greece, and it is still a popular tourist destination today.

More than 11,000 objects from the museum's collection span from early prehistory to late antiquity. Pottery, sculpture, jewelry, coinage, and other objects are shown in the displays, which provide a fascinating look into the vibrant history and culture of ancient Greece. The museum is split up into many parts, each of which focuses on a different component or era of ancient Greek civilization.

The Mycenaean Collection, which showcases artifacts from one of Greece's first civilizations, the Mycenaean, is among the museum's most remarkable parts. Being one of the most well-known relics from ancient Greece, the famed gold mask of Agamemnon is included in this collection together with other stunning examples of pottery, bronze, gold, and ivory.

The Classical Collection, another well-liked area of the museum, has a sizable number of objects from ancient Greece's classical era, including the well-known bronze figure of Zeus or Poseidon, the Antikythera mechanism, and the Marathon Boy. The Roman Collection at the museum is also highly noteworthy; it has a variety of antiquated Roman items, such as mosaics, frescoes, and sculptures.

Other significant collections housed at the museum include the Prehistoric Collection, the Egyptian and Near Eastern Collection, and the Vase and Small Items Collection. Many Greek vases from antiquity may be found in the Vase and Small Items Collection, along with other minor objects like jewelry and figurines. The Neolithic and Cycladic eras, as well as other early stages of Greek history, are the subject of the Prehistoric Collection. A variety of ancient items, including mummies, hieroglyphics, and other ancient artifacts, may be found in the museum's Egyptian and Near Eastern Collection, which is a more recent addition.

A must-visit location for anybody interested in the history and culture of ancient Greece is the National Archaeological Museum of Athens. It offers a fascinating look into the ancient world and the people who lived during that period because of its enormous collection of antiquated items and riches. The National Archaeological Museum is a very exceptional museum that you should not miss, whether you are an archaeology expert or just interested in Greek history.

The Benaki Museum

One of Greece's most significant museums, the Benaki Museum is situated in the heart of Athens. It was established in 1930 by renowned Greek art collector Antonis Benakis and today houses an extraordinary collection of works of art and artifacts that date from antiquity to the present period.

A stunning late 19th-century neoclassical structure that houses the museum was built. It was made into a museum when the Benakis family gave it to the Greek government in 1930. Originally, it served as their residence. The most recent makeover, which was finished in 2000, was one of several that the building has received throughout the years.

The collection of the Benaki Museum is split up into a number of distinct departments, each of which specializes in a certain era of Greek history. Around 45,000 objects, including Byzantine, Islamic, Chinese, and European art, as well as ancient Greek antiquities, may be found in the museum's collection.

The museum's collection of Greek antiquities is among its most stunning features. Pottery, sculpture, and other artifacts from the Bronze Age, Archaic, Classical, and Hellenistic periods are included in the museum's collection. The collection comprises a number of well-known items, including Mycenaean clay figures, a Corinthian helmet, and an Agamemnon burial mask.

The museum's collection of Byzantine and Christian art is extremely noteworthy, and it includes many icons, frescoes, and other religious artifacts. Objects from the early Christian era, the Byzantine Empire, and the post-Byzantine era are all represented in the collection.

The museum's collection of Islamic art is another significant component. Many Islamic civilizations, including Ottoman Turkey, Iran, and Egypt, are represented in the collection. The collection consists of a wide range of items, including textiles, metalwork, and pottery.

With many items from different eras in Chinese history, the museum's collection of Chinese art is highly remarkable. Ceramics, jade artifacts, and other ornamental arts are all part of the collection.

Moreover, there is a sizable collection of decorative arts, sculptures, and paintings from several European nations. Famous painters such as El Greco, Rembrandt, and Van Gogh have pieces in the collection.

During the year, the Benaki Museum also offers temporary exhibits in addition to its permanent collection. These shows often include items from other museums and collections and cover a variety of subjects relating to Greek history and culture.

Anybody who is interested in Greek art and culture must visit the Benaki Museum. The museum is a wonderful location to learn about the rich history of Greece and admire the beauty of Greek art because of its vast collection and lovely structure.

Other Museums and Cultural Attractions in Athens

In addition to the above Museum, Athens is home to a variety of other cultural attractions and museums. Here are a few more notable ones to consider visiting:

Museum of Cycladic Art: The art and culture of the Cyclades, a collection of Greek islands in the Aegean Sea, are the focus of this museum. Cycladic figures, antique pottery, and other relics are on display with current and modern Greek artwork.

Byzantine and Christian Museum: The early Christian era in Greece and the Byzantine Empire are the subjects of this museum's exhibits. Icons, mosaics, and other holy treasures are shown among everyday items like ceramics and textiles.

Stavros Niarchos Foundation Cultural Center: With a music hall, an opera theater, and a national library, this contemporary complex serves as Athens' cultural center. The building has excellent architecture and design, with an emphasis on sustainability and energy economy.

Museum of the City of Athens: This museum is housed in a historic mansion and has displays about Athens' history, from the prehistoric era to the present. The collection comprises a replica of a 19th-century Athens street together with maps, images, costumes, and other items.

Hellenic Motor Museum: The museum's collection of old and new automobiles, motorbikes, and other vehicles will appeal to automotive aficionados. Exotic and unusual vehicles from all around the globe are on show, together with interactive exhibits and multimedia presentations.

Museum of Islamic Art: With an emphasis on the Ottoman Empire and other Islamic civilizations that had an influence on Greece, this museum is devoted to the art and culture of the Islamic world. Together with religious relics and texts, the exhibits include ceramics, clothing, jewelry, and other items from everyday life.

Athens War Museum: This museum has displays on ancient warfare, the Byzantine Empire, the Ottoman Empire, and contemporary Greek history and is devoted to the history of the

Greek military. The exhibitions include the use of the Greek military in World War II and later wars, as well as weapons, uniforms, and other military relics.

Athens boasts an abundance of museums and cultural sites to visit, whether your interests are in ancient history, art, and culture, or more contemporary pastimes. Visitors are guaranteed to discover something that fascinates them and enhances their experience of this intriguing city with the abundance of alternatives available.

Part III: The Peloponnese

Chapter 6: Discovering the Peloponnese

Top Attractions in the Peloponnese

The Peloponnese is a peninsula in southern Greece that is rich in history, culture, and natural beauty. There are many top attractions in the region that are worth visiting. Here are some of the most popular:

Mycenae: The Mycenaean civilization, which lasted from the 16th to the 12th century BC, was originally centered in this ancient metropolis. The city is well-known for both its iconic Lion Gate and its strong defenses.

The Peloponnese area of Greece's ancient city of Mycenae is renowned for its historical importance and stunning architecture. The city served as the hub of the Mycenaean civilization, which is believed to have existed from the sixteenth and the twelfth centuries BC. Around 90 kilometers southwest of Athens, in the Peloponnese's Argolis area, is where you'll find Mycenae.

The Lion Gate, the city's main entrance, is among Mycenae's most well-known landmarks. The two lionesses that are engraved into the stone above the entrance gave the gate its name. The Lion Gate is often utilized as a symbol of the city and of the Mycenaean civilization and is regarded as one of the finest examples of ancient Greek architecture.

Mycenae is the location of several more stunning architectural marvels in addition to the Lion Gate. Impressive fortifications were constructed to encircle the city in order to keep intruders out. These fortifications are an incredible feat of engineering, constructed of enormous stones that are packed together without the use of mortar.

The tholos tomb also called the Treasury of Atreus, is one of Mycenae's most spectacular structures. The construction of this beehive-shaped tomb dates to the thirteenth century BC. One of the greatest technological feats of the Mycenaean civilization, the tomb is constructed of enormous stones that may weigh up to 120 tons.

The palace complex, which served as the political and religious hub of Mycenae, is another noteworthy aspect of the city. The Megaron, which served as the palace's principal hall, and the throne chamber, which was utilized for ceremonial occasions, are both included in the complex of the palace. The palace complex also has a number of courtyards and apartments used for storage, where food and other supplies were kept.

Mycenae is renowned for its extensive history and mythology in addition to its stunning architecture. Agamemnon, the king who commanded the Greek armies in the Trojan War, lived at Mycenae, which, according to tradition, was established by Perseus, the son of Zeus. The city is referenced in a number of ancient Greek tales as well, and it is said to have had a big impact on Greek civilization.

Mycenae is a well-liked tourist destination today and a must-see site for anybody interested in the history and architecture of ancient Greece. Visitors may visit the city and its stunning defenses, tombs, and palaces while learning about the Mycenaean civilization's rich history and mythology. Visitors may take a stroll around the hills and valleys that surround the city while admiring breathtaking views of the Peloponnese area. The city is also surrounded by lovely scenery.

Epidaurus: A theater from the fourth century BC is located at this historic location. The theater, which is still in use today for productions of classical Greek plays, is renowned for its extraordinary acoustics.

On the Greek Peloponnese peninsula's northeastern shore sits the historic city of Epidaurus. The site's well-preserved theater, which is regarded as one of the outstanding specimens of ancient Greek theater design, is what makes it most well-known. Both tourists and theater fans visit it often.

It is believed that the theater, which was constructed in the fourth century BC, could accommodate 14,000 people. Its exceptional acoustics, which is a hallmark of its architecture, permitted even those seated at the highest levels to hear the players on stage without the need for contemporary technology. Ancient Greek plays are being performed at the theater today, along with other cultural activities including concerts and festivals.

In addition to the theater, Epidaurus is also the location of various other historic structures, such as a stadium, a gymnasium, and a temple to the deity of healing Asclepius. It is believed that the sanctuary, which was a popular stop for pilgrims looking for remedies for their afflictions, is where modern medicine first emerged.

The natural environment of Epidaurus is among its most stunning features. The location provides breathtaking views of the surrounding countryside and is surrounded by verdant hills and valleys. Visitors may either climb into the neighboring mountains for a more difficult experience or enjoy a leisurely stroll around the ruins.

In addition to its cultural and historical importance, Epidaurus is a crucial location for comprehending the evolution of drama and theater in ancient Greece. The theater at Epidaurus is regarded as an engineering marvel, and its style has inspired theater design for ages. It continues to be a source of inspiration for theater fans and historians today and is a tribute to the inventiveness and brilliance of the ancient Greeks.

Anybody interested in the history, culture, or drama of the ancient Greeks must pay a visit to Epidaurus. It provides a special window into the past and a chance to take in Greece's breathtaking natural splendor. A vacation to Epidaurus is certain to be a once-in-a-lifetime experience, regardless of whether you are a seasoned tourist or a first-time visitor.

Monemvasia: The unusual location of Monemvasia provides travelers with a window into medieval Greece. A tiny causeway links the town's location on a small island to the mainland in the southeast Peloponnese. Because of its advantageous position and the formidable walls that surround it, it is often referred to as the "Gibraltar of the East."

The town was initially founded in the sixth century AD, and it has a lengthy history. It was governed by a variety of empires throughout the years, including the Byzantine, Venetian, and Ottoman. The town has the imprint of each dynasty, resulting in an intriguing fusion of architectural styles.

The ancient town, which is situated on the southern half of the island, is one of Monemvasia's primary attractions. The ancient town is a labyrinth of passageways and little streets that are dotted with stone homes and old-style Greek churches. The structures were constructed in the 13th and 14th centuries, and several have undergone exquisite restorations. The Byzantine stronghold, which is located at the summit of the hill and provides breathtaking views of the Aegean Sea, is the most spectacular structure in the ancient town.

The Church of Agia Sofia, one of the oldest and most spectacular churches in Greece, is another must-see site in Monemvasia. The church, which was constructed in the 13th century, is a stunning illustration of Byzantine design. It has exquisite mosaics, complex frescoes, and a magnificent dome supported by columns.

Monemvasia's lovely beaches, which include pristine seas and breathtaking views of the surrounding mountains, are also open to visitors. Pori Beach, which is situated on the western side of the island, and Ampelakia Beach, which is situated on the eastern side, are two of the most well-known beaches in the vicinity.

In addition to its stunning surroundings and fascinating past, Monemvasia is renowned for its top-notch regional food. The village is home to a multitude of traditional tavernas and eateries that provide delectable cuisine including fresh fish and local cheeses. Guests may try regional favorites including octopus in red wine sauce, roasted lamb with herbs, and creamy cheese pies.

Anybody interested in history, architecture, or stunning landscapes should go to Monemvasia. It is a genuinely distinctive and unforgettable location to visit in the Peloponnese because of its well-preserved medieval town, gorgeous beaches, and delicious local food.

Diros Caves: The Peloponnese's western shore is home to these magnificent limestone caverns. The amazing stalactites and stalagmites in the caverns may be seen by taking a boat trip.

On the western coast of the Peloponnese, on the Mani Peninsula, are the Diros Caves, which are sometimes referred to as the Pyrgos Dirou Caves. The caverns are well-known for their extraordinary subterranean lakes and beautiful stalactite and stalagmite formations.

A local shepherd made the first discovery of the caverns in the late 19th century, and since then they have gained popularity as a tourist attraction. The Diros Caves' subterranean chambers are filled with crystal-clear water that mirrors the surreal formations above, and visitors may take a boat excursion through them. During the boat trip, which lasts around 30 minutes, guests may take in the splendor of the caverns and discover more about their geology and history.

The Alepotrypa Cave, a sizable cavern with towering stalactites and stalagmites that mimic the columns of an old temple, is the first stop on the trip. Archaeological data indicates that the cave may have been utilized as a site of worship during the Neolithic era when it is thought that people lived there.

Visitors are guided into the Vlychada Cave, which has lakes and canals below ground, in the second portion of the journey. Due to its black tint, which is brought on by the lack of light, the biggest of these lakes, called the "Black Lake," earned its nickname. Together with formations of every size and shape, visitors may also view a little waterfall and a network of chambers and tunnels.

The astonishing variety of hues in the Diros Caves is one of its most outstanding characteristics. Pure white to deep red and hues of pink, orange, and yellow are among the formations seen in the caverns. The mineral composition of the limestone, which has been gradually dissolved and redeposited over thousands of years, is what gives the rocks their hues.

Visitors visiting the Diros Caves have the option of taking a boat trip or exploring the neighborhood, which is renowned for its gorgeous beaches and breathtaking coastal landscape. The surrounding village of Gythio is renowned for its picturesque port and classic Greek architecture, while the adjoining town of Areopoli is a nice spot to stop for a meal or a coffee.

In general, everybody traveling to the Peloponnese must see the Diros Caves. They provide a unique window into the area's natural splendor and geological past and are certain to make an impact on everyone who visits.

Nafplio: The Most Beautiful Town in Greece

Nafplio: Immediately after Greece's independence from the Ottoman Empire in the 19th century, this picturesque village served as the nation's first capital. The town has a lovely port as well as a number of old sites, such as the Bourtzi Castle and the Palamidi Fortress.

The Peloponnese's northern region has the charming town of Nafplio. Its history extends back to antiquity, and the Byzantine and Ottoman eras considered it an important hub. It served as Greece's first capital in the nineteenth century, after the country's independence from the Ottoman Empire. Nafplio is a well-liked tourist attraction nowadays because of its lovely port, gorgeous architecture, and fascinating past.

The Palamidi Fortress is one of Nafplio's most popular attractions. The castle, which was erected by the Venetians in the 18th century and is situated on a hill overlooking the town, was significant in the Greek War of Independence. Tourists may ascend the fortress's stairs for breathtaking views of the town and surroundings.

The Bourtzi Castle is another well-liked Nafplio tourist destination. The castle was erected by the Venetians in the 15th century and is situated on a tiny island in the harbor. It functioned as a stronghold to defend the town from invasions. Nowadays, tourists may take a quick boat journey to the island to view the castle and explore the surrounding area.

A must-see location in Nafplio is the ancient town. It's a lovely spot to stroll and explore, with streets lined with vibrant buildings and classic Greek architecture. The Church of Agios Spyridon, the Archaeological Museum, and the First Parliament Building of Greece are just a few of the historic sites in the town.

Syntagma Square, a large area surrounded by neoclassical buildings and outdoor cafés, is one of the attractions of the old town. It's a popular location for events and festivals and a wonderful place to unwind and take in the town's vibe.

Only a short drive from the town center, Nafplio is renowned for its stunning beaches. Karathona Beach, a lengthy stretch of sandy beach ideal for swimming and sunbathing, is one of the most well-liked beaches. Arvanitia Beach, which is just a short walk from the old town and provides breathtaking views of the sea and the surrounding mountains, is another well-liked beach.

With its extensive selection of authentic Greek cuisine, Nafplio is a fantastic destination for foodies. Many eateries and tavernas in the town sell grilled meats, fresh fish, and other regional delicacies. Also, there are several cafés and pastry stores where you may indulge in delectable Greek coffee and pastries.

The lovely city of Nafplio has much to offer everyone. Nafplio is a fantastic place to visit whether you want to relax on the beach, learn about architecture or both.

Ancient Olympia: The Birthplace of the Olympic Games

Ancient Olympia: The Olympic Games, which were staged every four years in Zeus' honor from the eighth century BC until the fourth century AD, originated at this location. The old stadium's remains, the Philippeion, the Temple of Zeus, and more are all still visible to tourists today.

The ancient stadium's remains may be explored by tourists that visit Ancient Olympia. The stadium, which can accommodate up to 45,000 people, was initially constructed in the sixth century BC. Visitors may stroll through the tunnel where the athletes would have entered the stadium and take in the breathtaking views of the surroundings. It is a very magnificent sight.

The Temple of Zeus, one of the biggest temples in ancient history, is another attraction in Ancient Olympia. It was constructed in the fifth century BC, and one of the Seven Wonders of the Ancient World, a huge statue of Zeus, was placed within. Visitors may still view the temple's remains, which include its majestic columns and pediments, even though the statue has since vanished.

Another intriguing building at the location is the Philippeion, which was erected by Philip II of Macedon to mark his victory in the Battle of Chaeronea in 338 BC. The circular structure is an amazing example of classical Greek architecture, and it is decorated with sculptures of Philip and other members of his family.

A variety of antiquities from the location are on display at the Archaeological Museum, which is open to visitors to Ancient Olympia. The Nike of Paionios, a monument of the goddess Nike that formerly stood at the entrance to the old stadium, and the Hermes of Praxiteles, a figure of the messenger god that is regarded as one of the greatest specimens of ancient Greek sculpture, are just a few of the highlights of the museum.

Visitors to Ancient Olympia may take in the region's breathtaking natural beauty in addition to its historical and cultural attractions. The property is situated in a beautiful valley surrounded by forested hills, and the region has a number of hiking paths that provide excellent views of the surroundings.

Anybody interested in the history and culture of ancient Greece must pay a visit to Ancient Olympia. The location provides a fascinating look into the old Olympic Games' culture and a rare chance to tour some of the most stunning historic ruins. A visit to Ancient Olympia is a once-in-a-lifetime experience, regardless of whether you're interested in history or you just want to take in the natural beauty of the Peloponnese.

Mani: The Land of Stone Towers

Mani Peninsula: The Mani Peninsula is a location of Greece's Peloponnese peninsula that lies to the south. It has a rough topography that encompasses both a mountainous interior and a dramatic coastline and is renowned for its breathtaking natural beauty. The area is renowned for its characteristic stone towers, which are found all over the place and bear witness to the particular history of the area.

From the beginning of time, people have lived on the Mani Peninsula, and its rich cultural past can be seen in the region's architecture, artwork, and rituals. The historic stone towers that dot the landscape are among the region's most recognizable characteristics. The local tribes who resided there used these towers as defensive fortifications throughout the Middle Ages. Several of these towers have been rebuilt and are again accessible to tourists, giving them a look into the distinctive history and culture of the area.

The Mani Peninsula is well-liked by outdoor lovers in addition to those interested in history and culture. Because of its rocky landscape, the area is a fantastic place to go trekking, with simple to difficult hikes. The Mani Trail, which connects the communities of

Lagada and Kardamyli and gives breathtaking views of the surrounding mountains and sea, is one of the most well-liked hiking trails.

Moreover, the Mani Peninsula is renowned for its stunning beaches with clean seas and fine sand. The most well-known beaches are those in Stoupa, Kalogria, and Kardamyli. Several of these beaches provide a variety of water activities, including kayaking, paddle boarding, and snorkeling, making them ideal for swimming, tanning, and resting.

The Mani Peninsula is home to a number of quaint towns and villages for visitors who are interested in seeing the area's traditional settlements. These little towns, with their typical stone homes, winding alleyways, and local markets, provide a look into the distinctive cultural history of the area. Areopoli, Vathia, and Gerolimenas are a few of the most well-liked settlements to visit.

The Mani Peninsula is a special location with stunning scenery that has plenty to offer everyone. There is much to see and do in this beautiful area of Greece, whether you are interested in learning about the area's history and culture, taking in the great outdoors, or just unwinding on the beach.

Chapter 7: The Greek Islands

Introduction to the Greek Islands

The Aegean and Ionian Seas in the eastern Mediterranean are home to more than 6,000 islands and islets together known as the Greek Islands. The Cyclades, the Dodecanese, the North Aegean Islands, the Sporades, the Ionian Islands, and the Saronic Islands are the six major groupings into which these islands are separated. They're well-known for their pure seas, stunning beaches, historic sites, and quaint towns and villages.

For a very long time, tourists looking for a blend of culture, history, and natural beauty have made their way to the Greek Islands. Every island has its own personality and draws, from Mykonos' party atmosphere to Santorini's enchanting sunsets. Tourists may spend their days relaxing on the beach, discovering historic sites, or just meandering through the little towns.

The Greek Islands are the perfect place to go if you want a relaxing vacation. There is a suitable island for everyone among the more than 200 inhabited islands available. There are a lot of characteristically Greek white-washed structures, blue-domed churches, and cobblestone alleys on several of the islands. The Greek Islands are a great choice whether you're searching for a romantic getaway, an action-packed vacation, or a family-friendly location.

The Cyclades, which include the famous islands of Mykonos and Santorini, is one of the most well-known island groupings. Mykonos is renowned for its vibrant nightlife, opulent lodgings, and international vibe. The island is known for drawing A-listers and jet-setters from all over the globe, and the beaches, eateries, and nightclubs all reflect this upscale ambiance.

On the other side, Santorini is renowned for its spectacular vistas, romantic ambiance, and breathtaking sunsets. The island is well-known for its blue-domed churches set on the rim of a volcanic crater and its whitewashed structures. Tourists may take a boat excursion to see the island's secret beaches and go swimming in the Aegean Sea's pristine waters.

The Ionian Islands, which are a popular island group, are found in western Greece. These islands include Kefalonia, Zakynthos, and Corfu, among others. The second-largest of the Ionian Islands, Corfu is renowned for its magnificent beaches, Venetian architecture, and verdant scenery. Navagio Beach, Zakynthos' blue caverns, and its thriving nightlife are all well-known. The biggest of the Ionian Islands, Kefalonia is renowned for its stunning coastline, clean seas, and medieval settlements.

Some of Greece's most beautiful and ancient islands are found in the Dodecanese Islands, which are part of the Aegean Sea's southeast region. The biggest Dodecanese island, Rhodes, is renowned for its historic Old Town, breathtaking beaches, and historic ruins. Hippocrates, the founder of modern medicine, was born at Kos, a Greek island famous for its idyllic towns and sandy beaches.

While less well-known than other island groups in the Aegean Sea, the North Aegean Islands are no less stunning. The mountain ranges on the island of Samos are recognized for their lush greenery, traditional towns, and historic sites. The third-largest island in Greece, Lesbos, is renowned for its charming towns, authentic food, and distinctive natural vistas.

The Saronic Islands are a series of islands that are close to Athens and are part of the Saronic Gulf. The islands of Aegina, Poros, Hydra, and Spetses are included in this collection. Although Poros is renowned for its lovely town and stunning beaches, Hydra is noted for its classic architecture and car-free streets.

The Greek Islands are famed not just for their exquisite natural beauty but also for their lengthy history and delectable food. Traditional foods including grilled meats, fresh fish, and feta cheese, as well as regional wines and spirits, are available to tourists.

The Greek Islands are the perfect location whether you're searching for a romantic break, a family holiday, or an action-packed excursion. Each island provides its own personality and attractions, and there are so many to select from that there is something for everyone.

The Cyclades: Mykonos and Santorini

A series of islands in the Aegean Sea called the Cyclades are renowned for their magnificent beaches, quaint communities, and distinctive cultures. Mykonos and Santorini are two of the Cyclades' several islands that are among the most well-liked and well-known.

The gorgeous landscape and exciting nightlife of Mykonos are well known. With its abundance of pubs, clubs, and beach parties, the island is well renowned for its vibrant party culture. The major settlement on the island, Chora, is a labyrinth of winding lanes dotted with whitewashed homes and vibrant bougainvillea. The town's many stores, eateries, and galleries may be explored by visitors, or they can choose to unwind on one of the island's many stunning beaches.

Mykonos is known for its beaches, nightlife, and several significant cultural landmarks. One of the most well-known is the stunning, whitewashed Church of Panagia Paraportiani in Chora. In reality, the church is a collection of chapels that were constructed over many centuries. For breathtaking views of the island and the surrounding sea, visitors may go to the top of the church's bell tower.

The Archaeological Museum of Mykonos is another well-liked cultural destination in Mykonos. A multitude of antique sculptures and pottery, as well as items from the Cycladic era, may be seen at this museum. As they tour the museum's many displays, visitors may discover more about the island's rich history and culture.

On the other side, Santorini is renowned for its enchanting ambiance and breathtaking sunsets. The island is well-known for its caldera, a large crater caused by volcanic activity thousands of years ago. Now that the caldera is filled with water, it has formed a magnificent natural harbor around towering cliffs and whitewashed homes.

See the various little towns in Santorini, each with its own distinct personality and attractions. One of the most well-known is Oia, a charming town situated on the island's northernmost point. Oia is renowned for its breathtaking caldera vistas, lovely whitewashed homes, and blue-domed churches.

The capital of the island, Fira, is another well-liked settlement on Santorini. Fira is a thriving community with plenty of stores, eateries, and cafés. Tourists may meander through the town's winding alleys and lanes or browse the town's many galleries and shops.

Santorini is home to numerous significant cultural landmarks in addition to its communities. The ancient Minoan city of Akrotiri, which was covered in ash after a volcanic eruption in the 17th century BCE, is one of the most well-known. The city's remains may be explored by visitors, and they include well-preserved structures, frescoes, and ceramics.

The Museum of Prehistoric Thira is another well-liked cultural destination in Santorini. A multitude of antique sculptures and pottery, as well as objects from the Minoan civilization, may be seen in this museum. As they tour the museum's many displays, visitors may discover more about the island's rich history and culture.

Anybody visiting Greece should make sure to see the Cyclades. Two of the most well-known and popular islands in the group are

Mykonos and Santorini, which are famed for their magnificent beaches, quaint towns, and rich cultures and histories. These islands have plenty to offer everyone, whether you're seeking wild nightlife or a quiet escape.

The Dodecanese: Rhodes and Kos

In the southeast Aegean Sea, there are 12 main islands and countless smaller islets that make up the Dodecanese group. The Minoans, Persians, Romans, Byzantines, Knights of Saint John, Ottomans, and Italians are just a few of the civilizations that have influenced the islands' rich history throughout the years. Rhodes and Kos, two of the most popular islands in the Dodecanese, each provide a unique fusion of history, culture, and scenic beauty.

The biggest island in the Dodecanese, Rhodes is renowned for its rich history, magnificent medieval buildings, and beautiful beaches. The city of Rhodes was one of the biggest and richest in the ancient Greek world, and the island was a significant center of civilization at the time. Visitors may now tour the spectacular Acropolis of Rhodes, the Temple of Apollo, and the Stadium among the old city's ruins. With its well-preserved medieval walls and structures, such as the Palace of the Grand Master of the Knights of Rhodes, the Knights' Hospital, and the Knights' Street, the Old Town of Rhodes is also a popular tourist destination. Walking through the Old

Town's winding lanes and alleyways, which is a UNESCO World Heritage Site, is like traveling back in time.

In addition to having a long history, Rhodes has some of Greece's most stunning beaches. Every style of beachgoer will find something here, from rocky coves and isolated bays to sandy beaches with pristine seas. The most well-known beaches are Anthony Quinn Bay, Tsambika, Lindos, and Faliraki.

Kos, on the other hand, is a lesser-known Dodecanese island that is renowned for its breathtaking natural landscape, quaint towns, and historic ruins. The history of the island is extensive and diverse, with Greek, Roman, Byzantine, Knights of Saint John, Ottoman, and Italian influences. The Asklepion, a prehistoric medical facility honoring the deity of medicine, Asklepios, is the most well-known location on the island. On a hilltop above Kos, the Asklepion ruins are home to breathtaking views of the surrounding landscape.

Kos is renowned for its stunning beaches, which have extensive lengths of sand and clear blue seas. The most well-known beaches are Paradise Beach, Mastichari, and Tigaki. The island is also home to a variety of quaint settlements, such as Kefalos, a typical fishing hamlet with a magnificent beach and a bustling nightlife, and Zia, a gorgeous mountain village with breathtaking views of the island and the sea.

Kos is a fantastic destination for foodies, offering a range of traditional Greek cuisine and fresh fish, in addition to its natural beauty and historic ruins. Moussaka, dolmades, tzatziki, and fresh fish grilled on the grill are a few of the regional favorites.

From Athens and other adjacent islands, ferries go directly to both Rhodes and Kos. These are excellent locations for tourists seeking to experience the finest of the Greek Islands since they provide a distinctive combination of history, culture, and natural beauty.

The Ionian Islands: Corfu and Zakynthos

Off Greece's western coast, in the Ionian Sea, lie the Ionian Islands. They are a well-liked vacation spot recognized for their luxuriant vegetation, stunning beaches, and pure seas. The islands have a long history and rich culture that have been influenced by several empires, notably the Venetian, French, and British. Corfu and Zakynthos are two of the Ionian group's most visited islands.

The second-largest island in the Ionian group is Corfu, which is often referred to as Kerkyra. Off Greece's northwest coast, it is renowned for its breathtaking beaches, Venetian-style buildings, and extensive history. Having been governed by the Venetians, the French, the Brits, and the Greeks, the island has a lengthy and varied history. The food, music, and architecture of the island all reflect its distinctive cultural past.

The Old Town, a UNESCO World Heritage site, is one of Corfu's primary attractions. The Liston, a lovely promenade with arches and cafés that is evocative of Venice, is one of the town's many examples of Venetian-style architecture. The Venetians constructed the Old Fortress in the town in the fifteenth century to defend it from invaders.

The Achilleion Palace, a stunning neoclassical structure that served as Empress Elisabeth of Austria's summer residence, is another well-liked destination on the island. The palace is well-known for its stunning gardens, monuments, and sea vistas.

The third-largest island in the Ionian group is Zakynthos, which is often referred to as Zante. It is a region off the west coast of Greece that is renowned for its breathtaking beaches, crystal-clear seas, and picturesque scenery. With occupations by the Greeks, French, British, and Venetians, the island has a lengthy and colorful history.

Navagio Beach, commonly known as Shipwreck Beach, is one of the primary attractions in Zakynthos. The rusty wreckage of a smuggler's ship that washed up on the shore in 1980 and this magnificent cove's crystal-clear waters are what make them famous. Only by boat, although the journey is well worth it for the breathtaking vistas and natural beauty, is it possible to reach the beach.

The Blue Caves, a group of sea caverns renowned for its crystal-clear blue waters and magnificent rock formations, are another well-liked destination on the island. The amazing colors and patterns of the rocks and water may be seen when taking a boat journey to explore the caverns.

Zakynthos is renowned for its extensive cultural legacy in addition to its natural beauty. The island is home to a number of historic villages, such as Keri and Volimes, both of which are well-known for their gorgeous stone homes and breathtaking sea vistas. Volimes is noted for its needlework.

A combination of natural beauty and cultural legacy can be found in the Ionian Islands, a stunning and intriguing travel destination. Just two of the several islands in the group, each with its own distinctive features and attractions, are Corfu and Zakynthos. The Ionian Islands provide something for everyone, whether you're seeking breathtaking beaches, historic sites, or charming towns.

Chapter 8: Transportation in Greece

Getting Around Athens

Getting around Athens is relatively easy and convenient, thanks to its modern transportation infrastructure. There are several options available to visitors, including public transportation, taxis, and rental cars.

Public Transportation:

Buses, the metro, and trams are all part of the enormous public transit infrastructure of Athens. With three lines that serve the majority of the city's key locations and attractions, the metro is the fastest method to get about the region. Also trustworthy and reasonably priced choices are the buses and trams, which have regular itineraries and operate day and night.

Athens' metro system is hygienic, effective, and contemporary. The Green Line (Line 1), the Red Line (Line 2), and the Blue Line are its three lines (Line 3). Each line includes a number of stations that cover most of the important landmarks and areas in the city. On weekdays, the metro operates from 5:30 am to midnight, while on weekends, it operates from 5:30 am to 2:00 am. A one-way ticket costs €1.40, while a 24-hour pass costs €4.50.

Athens has a sizable bus network as well, with several lines that go all over the city. The air-conditioned buses often operate from 5:00 am until midnight. A one-way ticket costs €1.40, while a 24-hour pass costs €4.50.

Taxis:

Athens residents often use taxis as a means of transportation, and they are simple to hail on the street or locate at taxi stands located all around the city. For visitors who wish to move about Athens quickly and conveniently, taxis are a practical alternative since they are often secure, dependable, and reasonably priced.

All cabs in Athens have meters, and the Greek government sets their prices. The initial cost of a taxi journey is normally in the range of

1.19 euros, and the cost per kilometer varies based on the time of day and the location from 0.68 to 1.19 euros. In addition, there are extra fees for items like baggage, tolls, and airport pickup.

The meter should be switched on at the beginning of the journey so that you are charged the right price. It's crucial to know that some dishonest taxi drivers may attempt to overcharge visitors. In order to avoid being led on a longer, more costly route, it is also a good idea to have a broad notion of the path you should follow toward your goal.

In Athens, you may utilize a number of taxi applications in addition to flagging down cabs on the street. If you don't have cash on hand, these applications provide you the option to order a cab and pay via the app. Beat, TaxiBeat, and Uber are a few of the most well-liked taxi applications in Athens.

While certain taxis may include a fold-down seat that may accommodate a fifth passenger, Athens legislation stipulates that taxis can only hold a maximum of four people. It's also important to keep in mind that certain Athens cabs have wheelchair elevators, albeit these may not always be accessible.

Although using a cab is often a safe and practical method to move about Athens, there are a few things to remember to make the journey go more smoothly. To pay for your journey, for instance, you need to make sure you have the right amount of change or a credit card, since some drivers may not have enough coins on hand. While some drivers may not understand English, it's also a good idea to have your destination written down or set up on your phone.

In conclusion, taxis are a practical and reasonably priced method to move about Athens, and they are extensively accessible all around the city. Although it's vital to be wary of the possibility of overcharging, the majority of taxi drivers are trustworthy and able to provide a convenient and pleasant means of transportation from one location to another.

Renting a Car in Greece

For those who wish to see Athens and its surroundings at their own leisure, renting a vehicle is a popular choice. Visitors may choose from a large selection of automobiles, including budget cars, SUVs, and luxury cars, from one of the many car rental agencies spread out over the city. Driving in Athens may be difficult, particularly for tourists who are not used to doing so in crowded cities.

A terrific method to get to Athens and see the neighboring places at your own speed is to rent a vehicle. You have the freedom to go to attractions outside the city without depending on scheduled excursions or public transit when you hire a vehicle. Athens is home to a number of automobile rental services, including both national and local businesses.

It's essential to be familiar with local driving laws and standards before hiring a vehicle. Drivers in Greece must be at least 21 years old and in possession of a current driver's license. Also, if you're not from the EU, you must have an international driving permit (IDP). It's a good idea to inquire about any extra conditions or limitations with the rental vehicle agency.

It's crucial to get acquainted with local driving habits and road conditions after you've leased a vehicle. As in much of Greece, Athens has some aggressive drivers who may not always abide by the rules of the road. It's critical to drive defensively and to be ready for lane changes that happen quickly and unpredictable driving. It's crucial to be careful and travel at a reasonable pace since Greek roads may sometimes be congested and twisting, particularly in rural regions.

Having the freedom to go outside of Athens is one of the main benefits of renting a vehicle. The historic remains of Delphi and the beach village of Sounion, which is the location of the Temple of Poseidon, are two-day outings that are readily accessible by automobile. Having a vehicle makes it simple to visit the surrounding Athens Riviera's villages and beaches, like Vouliagmeni and Glyfada.

Athens may be a difficult city for vehicles to park in. Particularly in the city center, parking spaces are few and sometimes difficult to locate. There is street parking accessible, although it often costs money at a parking meter. Since parking citations may be expensive, it's crucial to be informed of the parking policies in the area where you are parked.

Insurance is another thing to think about when renting a vehicle. The majority of rental vehicle agencies include a basic insurance package, but it's crucial to thoroughly study the terms and conditions and consider getting extra protection if necessary. To prevent getting penalized for damages later, it's a good idea to properly check the automobile before renting it and record any existing damage.

Getting a rental vehicle in Athens might be a terrific way to see the city and its surroundings. Driving in Athens can be a lucrative and fun experience with a little planning and prudence.

Bikes and Scooters:

Bikes and scooters may be rented in Athens for tourists who want a more environmentally friendly and physically active means of transportation. Visitors may hire either conventional bikes or electric bikes from any of the city's many bike rental businesses. There are various businesses that provide a variety of scooters for hire, catering to a variety of tastes.

Especially in the summer when it's nice and sunny, biking and scootering are excellent ways to move about Athens. Even though the city has some areas that are quite hilly, you can still get around on a bike or a scooter as long as you are familiar with the surroundings and the flow of traffic.

In Athens, you can hire bikes everywhere, and there are a lot of guided bike tours that take you throughout the city. With professional guides guiding the way, these excursions are a terrific way to see the city's diverse districts and attractions. The excursions can last anywhere from a few hours to a whole day and frequently stop at well-known locations like the Acropolis and the Ancient Agora.

Athens also offers scooter rentals, with several merchants providing both day and weekly rentals. In comparison to guided tours or public transportation, scooters are a popular option for people who want to explore the city on their own terms. Scooter riders should use caution and familiarize themselves with the traffic laws before leaving the house because Athens' traffic can be quite chaotic.

One of the main advantages of biking or scootering in Athens is that you can explore the city at your own pace and find off-the-beaten-path gems. Many of the city's most fascinating neighborhoods and attractions can be reached by bike or scooter but are difficult to reach by car or public transportation. For instance, it is best to explore the

Exarchia and Psyrri neighborhoods on foot or by bicycle because they are known for their vibrant street art and alternative culture.

Another benefit of bicycling or scootering in Athens is that it is a reasonably inexpensive and environmentally friendly mode of transportation. Since they produce no pollution, bicycles, and scooters can help cities cut down on traffic jams and carbon emissions. A bike or scooter rental is also typically much less expensive than a taxi or other modes of transportation.

However, it's crucial to be knowledgeable about the possible dangers of biking and scootering in Athens. The city's streets can be congested and cramped, and it's possible that drivers aren't always alert to a scooter or bicycle rider. Moreover, some of the city's hills can be steep and difficult to ride up, especially for inexperienced riders.

Overall, riding a bike or a scooter is a great way to get around Athens and can be a fun and interesting way to see the city. You'll have an unforgettable experience whether you decide to go on a guided bike tour, rent a scooter for the day, or just go exploring on your own. Just remember to exercise caution and maintain your safety as you move through the crowded city streets.

Walking:

And finally, if you're in the historic part of Athens, walking is a great way to get around. The Acropolis, the Ancient Agora, and the Temple of Olympian Zeus are just a few of the city's top sights that can all be reached on foot. The city's charming neighborhoods and streets can also be explored by visitors, who can pause at various cafes, eateries, and shops along the way. Athens can be hilly, and there are some places where the sidewalks are uneven, so keep that in mind.

In the city center, where many of Athens' top attractions are situated close to one another, walking is a great way to get around the city. Walking is a practical and effective way to get around Athens because of its small size, as you can avoid traffic and parking hassles.

The Plaka historic district is one of the best places in Athens for walking. At the base of the Acropolis, there is a charming neighborhood with winding streets and alleys lined with colorful homes, boutiques, and tavernas. You can see examples of the traditional Greek way of life and architecture while strolling through Plaka. It's also a great place to buy gifts, get a snack or meal, or just take in the atmosphere.

The National Garden is another well-liked location for strolling. This urban oasis in the middle of Athens offers a tranquil retreat from the city's hustle and bustle and is situated right behind the Parliament building. There are numerous ponds, fountains, small ruins, and different kinds of trees and plants in the garden. It's a wonderful location for a leisurely stroll, a picnic, or just to unwind.

Philopappos Hill is a must-see location for people who like long walks. This hill provides expansive views of the city and the sea and is situated just southwest of the Acropolis. You can either ascend the historic steps that lead to the top or one of the numerous hiking trails that wind through the park to get there. The Philopappos Monument, a palatial tomb constructed in the second century AD for a Roman politician, is located on the summit and is a great location to view the city's sunsetting.

Athens also provides a variety of guided walking tours, which are a wonderful way to see the city with the assistance of an informed guide. These tours can give you a deeper understanding of the city and its culture because they can be tailored to a variety of themes, including food, history, architecture, or street art.

Walking around Athens is a convenient and enjoyable activity, but it's important to be cautious and aware of your surroundings, especially in crowded areas or at night. Athens can be hot and muggy, especially in the summer, so it's a good idea to dress comfortably and carry a water bottle.

Ferry and Flight Options for Island Hopping

Greece has several ferry and airplane alternatives for island hopping, and they provide a wonderful opportunity to visit the various islands that make up this beautiful nation. Island hopping is a well-liked method to discover the distinctive culture, environments, and histories of each island, and there are more than 6,000 of them.

In Greece, ferries are the most popular means of transportation for island hopping. With various ferry companies offering services between the islands, the Greek ferry system is large, dependable, and reasonably priced. The three major ferry operators are Aegean Speed Lines, Hellenic Seaways, and Blue Star Ferries. Ferries come in a variety of sizes and grades, with choices ranging from budget-friendly to opulent. Although the smaller boats provide a more regional and genuine experience, the bigger ships often contain restaurants, cafés, and stores aboard.

It is important to check the websites of the ferry companies for the most recent information since ferry timetables and costs might change depending on the time of year. To avoid long lines and fully booked boats, it's also a good idea to purchase your tickets in advance, particularly during the busy summer months of July and

August. The boat voyage might take anything from a few hours to a whole day, depending on how far apart the islands are. Athens to Mykonos, Athens to Santorini, and Mykonos to Santorini are some of the busier boat routes.

There are other airplane choices for individuals who want to go between the islands more quickly. Olympic Air and Aegean Airlines are the two primary airlines that fly between the major islands and Athens. Generally speaking, flights are more costly than ferries, but they may also save you time and energy, particularly if you're going a long way. Although flights between the islands may take as little as 15 minutes, flights between Athens and the islands often last 45 to an hour.

The ferry and aircraft timetables, as well as the transportation requirements to and from the ports and airports, should all be taken into account while organizing your island-hopping itinerary. Sometimes, staying an extra night in Athens may be necessary in order to catch an early boat or flight. Moreover, it's a good idea to reserve lodging in advance, particularly during the peak season when many of the well-liked islands may become congested and pricey.

There is a lot to see and learn when island hopping in Greece, making it a special and rewarding experience. You will have the chance to enjoy the varied landscapes, food, and cultures of each island, whether you decide to go by boat or fly, creating experiences that will last a lifetime.

In conclusion, Athens provides a variety of practical and economical mobility alternatives, including taxis, rental vehicles, bikes, scooters, public transit, and walking. The option that best satisfies a visitor's requirements and tastes may be selected, allowing them to experience the city at their own speed.

Part IV: Northern Greece

Chapter 9: Exploring Northern Greece

Thessaloniki: Greece's Second City

Greece's second-largest city and its cultural center is Thessaloniki. It is a dynamic and historical city that is situated on the Aegean Sea coast in the Central Macedonia area of northern Greece. The city is the ideal fusion of the historic past, Byzantine and Ottoman architecture, contemporary conveniences, and a vibrant social scene. This is a thorough guide to Thessaloniki, the second-largest city in Greece.

History

When King Cassander of Macedonia built Thessaloniki in 315 BC, it began a long and rich history. Throughout history, the city has served as a strategic site and has been governed by many peoples, including the Romans, the Byzantines, and the Ottoman Turks. Thessaloniki has seen several earthquakes and fires, yet each time the city has been rebuilt and has kept most of its ancient structures and architecture.

Sightseeing

There are several interesting historical sites and attractions in Thessaloniki. The most well-known of them is the White Tower, a municipal emblem and significant historical landmark. The Ottomans constructed the White Tower in the fifteenth century, and it now serves as home to a museum that chronicles the history of the city.

The Byzantine Walls, which were constructed in the fourth century AD and acted as a protective barrier for the city, are another well-liked landmark in Thessaloniki. Parts of the walls still exist and are accessible to tourists today. A number of churches and monasteries are also located in the city, notably the well-known Hagios Demetrios, which is devoted to the city's patron saint.

Culture

The various museums and galleries in Thessaloniki represent the city's rich cultural legacy. There are several theaters and music venues located all across the city, which boasts a thriving cultural culture. Every November, Thessaloniki hosts the International Film Festival, which draws movie buffs from all over the globe.

Food and Drink

Thessaloniki is a culinary haven known for its delectable food and wine. There are several eateries, taverns, and cafés in the city that provide anything from Greek specialties to food from across the world. The city is renowned for its regional foods, including cheese, wine, and olives.

Nightlife

There are several pubs, clubs, and music venues in Thessaloniki, which has a thriving nightlife. There are several live music venues spread out around the city, which boasts a thriving music culture.

Thessaloniki has plenty to offer whether you're searching for a night of dancing or a casual drink with pals.

Shopping

Thessaloniki is a fantastic place to go shopping, with a variety of boutiques, stores, and marketplaces to check out. There are several traditional crafts and souvenirs that can be obtained at the markets and stores located all across the city, which is known for its leather items and jewelry.

Getting Around

Thessaloniki is a fairly walkable city, and many of the major landmarks and tourist attractions are close to one another. An excellent public transportation infrastructure connects the city to other regions of Greece through buses and trains. Those who want to drive may alternatively use taxis or hire a vehicle.

Visitors may find a number of attractions in the lively, ancient city of Thessaloniki. Anybody who wants to experience the rich history, stunning architecture, delectable cuisine and drink, and vibrant social scene of Greece should visit this city.

Meteora: The Monasteries on the Rocks

In the center of Greece, close to the town of Kalambaka, lies a unique geological phenomenon called Meteora. It is made up of a collection of massive rock formations that soar up to 400 meters (1,300 feet) above the plain below. The Meteora Monasteries, a collection of Eastern Orthodox monasteries, are located among these granite pillars.

The first hermits arrived in the region in the eleventh century looking for solitude and a means to commune with God. This is when the Meteora Monasteries were founded. Initially residing in natural rock fissures and caverns, these hermits then started to construct churches and monasteries. The monasteries were constructed over a number of centuries and served the local populace as institutions of learning and spirituality.

The Great Meteoron, the Holy Trinity, the Varlaam, St. Stephen, the Roussanou, and the St. Nicholas Anapafsas are the six active monasteries in Meteora at the moment. All of them sit atop the imposing granite pillars and may be reached through steps cut out of the rock or a system of pulleys and ropes for moving people and things.

The Great Meteoron, which dates to the fourteenth century, is the biggest and oldest of the monasteries. A steep flight of stairs leads up to it, which is perched on the tallest granite pillar. A substantial collection of historic books, paintings, and artifacts are kept at the monastery.

Another renowned monastery, The Holy Trinity, is set on a 400-meter (1,300-foot) high granite pillar. It may be reached by way of a precarious bridge and many steep stairs. Visitors can see all the way to the Pindus Mountains from the monastery, which is renowned for its stunning views of the surroundings.

On a smaller rock pillar, the Varlaam Monastery is situated, and it is reached via a bridge that crosses a narrow ravine. A magnificent collection of icons, frescoes, and other artifacts may be discovered there, which was established in the middle of the fourteenth century.

The lone rock pillar that is linked to the mainland is where you will find the St. Stephen Monastery, making it the most accessible. The little museum there, which was created in the 16th century, has a collection of religious objects.

A bridge connects to the Roussanou Monastery, which is perched on a smaller rock pillar. It was established in the 16th century and has a tiny chapel as well as a number of paintings.

The St. Nicholas Anapafsas monastery is the smallest of the group and is situated on a 40-meter-tall (130-foot-tall) granite pillar. It was established in the fourteenth century and is renowned for its stunning icons and paintings.

A unique experience, visiting the Meteora Monasteries combines faith, history, and spectacular natural beauty. Visitors are welcome at the monasteries, and a number of travel companies provide escorted excursions across the region.

In addition to the monasteries, Meteora is a well-liked location for trekking and rock climbing. Several hiking paths are available in the region, ranging in complexity from pleasant strolls to strenuous hikes that lead tourists right into the center of the rock formations. For tourists of all ability levels, the region is home to a number of climbing schools that provide guided climbing trips.

In conclusion, anybody visiting Greece should make time to visit the Meteora Monasteries. They provide a fascinating look into the nation's religious and cultural past, and the region's natural beauty is absolutely beautiful. Meteora has plenty to offer everyone, whether you are interested in spirituality, history, or outdoor adventure.

Mount Olympus: The Home of the Gods

Greece's tallest peak, Mount Olympus, rises 2,917 meters (9,570 feet) above sea level, dominating the surrounding area. Greek mythology describes it as the residence of the gods and goddesses, who live on its summit and conduct business in a palatial hall made of marble and gold. It is a location with significant cultural importance in Greek culture and has long been a favorite of hikers, mountaineers, and those interested in mythology.

Mount Olympus, which can be found in Greece's north, is a portion of the Olympus Range, which straddles the boundary between Macedonia and Thessaly. Both residents and visitors like taking day trips to the mountain, which is visible from the adjacent city of Thessaloniki. The summit is often covered in clouds, lending it a sense of mystery and intrigue. It is encircled by thick woods and rocky slopes, which provide breathtaking landscapes.

Because of its distinctive ecological and cultural value, Mount Olympus has been designated a UNESCO World Heritage Site. More than 1,700 plant species, many of which are unique to the area, as well as a number of animal species, such as wolves, deer, and wild boar, may be found on the mountain. The mountain has long been the focus of mythology, literature, and art, and it is a significant cultural place.

The story of the 12 Olympian gods and goddesses is among the most well-known tales connected to Mount Olympus. Zeus, the ruler of the gods, supposedly resided on Mount Olympus' summit with his wife Hera, as well as other deities including Poseidon, Athena, and Aphrodite. The gods were revered by the ancient Greeks for hundreds of years since they were thought to have created the world and governed the elements.

Mount Olympus is now a well-liked vacation spot for hikers and mountaineers. There are several routes leading to the mountain's top, which contains more than 50 peaks, the tallest of which is Mytikas. The E4 track, which begins in Litochoro and ascends the mountain through a series of treacherous switchbacks, is the most well-known route. While the trek is difficult and demands a high degree of fitness, the views from the summit make the effort worthwhile.

There are also various cable cars that provide a more leisurely climb for those who might prefer a less taxing alternative. The most well-known cable car runs from Katerini, a local village, up to Elatochori, a ski resort with breathtaking views of the surrounding peaks and valleys.

No matter the way you decide to experience Mount Olympus, you will undoubtedly have a memorable experience there. It is a natural marvel due to its soaring peaks and rugged beauty, and it exudes mystery and intrigue due to its rich cultural history and mythology. A trip to Mount Olympus is a must-do experience for everyone who enjoys hiking, the outdoors, or history.

Chapter 10: The Northern Greek Coastline

Halkidiki: The Three-Fingered Peninsula

Thessaloniki, Greece's second-largest city, lies around 100 kilometers away from the northern Greek peninsula of Halkidiki. It is well-known for its breathtaking coastline, lovely beaches, and pure seas. Due to its form, which resembles a hand with three fingers—Kassandra, Sithonia, and Mount Athos—, Halkidiki is often called the "three-fingered peninsula."

The most visited tourist attraction is Kassandra, which is located on the westernmost point of the Halkidiki peninsula. Sani, Kallithea, and Afytos are just a few of the gorgeous beaches there, along with a number of fascinating traditional towns. The picturesque hills and woodlands that surround the peninsula, as well as various ancient monuments like the Temple of Ammon Zeus, are open to visitors visiting Kassandra.

The Halkidiki peninsula's center finger, Sithonia, is renowned for its beautiful beaches and crystalline seas. In addition to various stunning environmental reserves and parks, including the Porto Koufo Marine Reserve and the Sithonia National Park, visitors to Sithonia may explore the picturesque fishing towns that dot the coastline. On Sithonia, Kavourotripes, Nikiti, and Toroni beaches are well-liked.

The Halkidiki peninsula's easternmost point, Mount Athos, is a UNESCO World Heritage site renowned for its magnificent monasteries and unmatched natural beauty. Several lovely beaches, like Ouranoupolis, can be found on Mount Athos, and tourists may take a boat excursion to view the monasteries from the sea.

Halkidiki is renowned for its mouthwatering regional cuisine, which includes fresh seafood, locally produced veggies, and traditional Greek meals, in addition to its magnificent coastline and natural beauty. Greek classics like moussaka, souvlaki, and Greek salads are available for tourists visiting Halkidiki to enjoy, along with regional delicacies like honey, olives, and wine.

Thessaloniki residents have a variety of transportation choices to go to Halkidiki. From the airport, guests may take a bus, or a cab, or hire a vehicle to drive themselves around the peninsula. For people who want to visit the adjacent islands, there are several ferry and boat services accessible.

Halkidiki is a lovely place with a blend of the natural world, history, and culture. Halkidiki is a must-see location in Northern Greece whether you want to unwind on the beach, discover quaint towns, or savor delectable Greek food.

The Prespa Lakes: A Natural Wonder

On the borders of Greece, Albania, and North Macedonia lies a group of three lakes known as the Prespa Lakes. They are located in the Prespa National Park, a place of exceptional ecological importance and natural beauty. The Greater Prespa Lake, the Smaller Prespa Lake, and the Mikri Prespa Lake are the three lakes that make up the Prespa Lakes.

The Greater Prespa Lake, which spans a region of around 285 square kilometers, is the biggest of the three lakes. It is surrounded by stunning mountains and trees and is located at an elevation of 853 meters. Several tributaries, notably the Devoll River, feed the lake, which empties into the Lesser Prespa Lake. A smaller lake, the Little Prespa Lake has a size of around 44 square kilometers. It is located at an elevation of 849 meters, and the water from the Greater Prespa Lake supplies its water supply. The Mikri Prespa Lake, with a surface area of around 48 square kilometers, is the smallest of the three lakes. It is located at an elevation of 853 meters and receives water from the Greater Prespa Lake as well.

A sanctuary for biodiversity and a natural treasure, the Prespa Lakes. More than 260 kinds of birds, many of them uncommon and endangered, may be found in the lakes and the surroundings around them. Water species like pelicans, herons, and cormorants who utilize the lakes as a stopover on their migratory routes value the region greatly. A number of fish species, notably the Prespa trout, which is unique to these lakes, are also found in the lakes.

There are various historic settlements in the region around the Prespa Lakes, each with its own distinct personality and charms. Agios Germanos, Laimos, and Psarades stand out among these settlements as the most significant. On the slopes of Mount Varnous, Agios Germanos is a charming town with a view of the Greater Prespa Lake. Several homes in the town were constructed in traditional Macedonian architecture, and the community has a long history. On the edge of Little Prespa Lake sits the lovely town of Laimos. The community is renowned for its lovely beach and mouthwatering seafood eateries. A little fishing community called Psarades may be found on the Mikri Prespa Lakc's edge. The hamlet is renowned for its mouthwatering fish dishes and beautiful stone homes.

Visitors may engage in a variety of activities at the Prespa Lakes, including birding, hiking, swimming, and fishing. There are several hiking paths that pass through the picturesque mountains and woods that surround the lakes. A terrific way to see the region's abundant biodiversity up close is to take a boat trip to the lakes, which are available to visitors. There are several fishing lodges and campsites around the lakes, which are also well-liked locations for fishing.

From numerous adjacent cities, including Florina, Kastoria, and Ioannina, the Prespa Lakes are readily accessible. There are many places to stay in the neighborhood, from modest guesthouses and bed and breakfasts to large hotels and resorts. Visitors are urged to appreciate the lakes' pristine beauty and take precautions to preserve the area's fragile environment.

Visitors to Greece should not pass up the chance to see the Prespa Lakes, which are stunning natural marvels. The lakes and the lands around them are home to a diverse group of traditional villages, each with its own personality and charms, as well as a rich biodiversity. Visitors may engage in a variety of activities at the lakes, including birding, hiking, swimming, and fishing. Whether you like the outdoors, are interested in history, or are just seeking a stunning and tranquil setting to unwind, the Pré

Kavala: A Hidden Gem on the Aegean Sea

On the Aegean Sea, in northern Greece, lies the city of Kavala. It is a hidden treasure that is sometimes disregarded by tourists and is known for its breathtaking architecture, extensive history, and gorgeous beaches. In this tour, we'll look at some of the top attractions in Kavala, including historic sites, breathtaking natural features, and cutting-edge services.

The architecture of Kavala is one of its most outstanding aspects. The city is perched on a hill and has meandering lanes that provide stunning views of the ocean and the countryside beyond. Panagia, the city's ancient district, is a tangle of colorful homes and cobblestone streets, many of which were built during the Ottoman period. Tourists may stroll through the winding alleyways and take in the distinctive fusion of Greek and Turkish architecture before stopping at one of the numerous cafés and tavernas to take it all in.

The Kavala Castle, a Byzantine castle from the sixth century AD, is located in the center of Panagia. The Byzantines, Venetians, Ottomans, and Greeks have all held the fortress at various points in its long and colorful history. Visitors may now stroll inside the castle's walls and towers while taking in the expansive views of the city and the ocean.

The Imaret, an Ottoman-era structure that once housed a Muslim theological school and hospice, is another important relic in Kavala. Although the Imaret is now a deluxe hotel and restaurant, guests are still welcome to explore its elaborate architecture and lovely garden.

Kavala also has a lot to offer people who are interested in ancient history. Just outside of the present-day city was the significant Hellenistic and Roman cultural hub of Philippi. Visitors may see the stunning remains of the Egnatia Road, a crucial Roman route that linked the east and west of the empire, as well as the remnants of the old theater, agora, and Forum.

Indeed, a trip to the beach is a must-do on any vacation to Kavala. There are numerous lovely beaches in the city, including the well-liked Batis and Tosca beaches. Swim in the pristine seas, take a stroll on the smooth beach or engage in water sports like windsurfing and kiteboarding while there.

Last but not least, Kavala is renowned for its delectable food, which combines Turkish and Greek tastes to provide a distinctive gastronomic experience. Fresh fish, flavorful meats, classic meals like moussaka and souvlaki, as well as regional specialties like bougatsa, a sweet pastry filled with custard or cheese, are available for tourists to consume.

As Kavala is close to an international airport and is readily accessible by car and bus from other regions of Greece, getting there is simple. While there, tourists may explore the area on foot or by bicycle because automobiles are not recommended due to the city's narrow streets and steep slopes.

In conclusion, the Aegean Sea city of Kavala is a hidden treasure that has something to offer everyone. This city is a must-visit location for any visitor wishing to enjoy the rich culture and natural beauty of Greece, from its spectacular architecture and historical buildings to its gorgeous beaches and mouthwatering food.

Chapter 11: Safety and Security Tips for Traveling in Greece

General Safety Tips for Traveling in Greece

Greece is a relatively safe country for travelers, but it's always important to take precautions to ensure your trip is trouble-free. Here are some general safety tips to keep in mind when traveling in Greece.

Keep an Eye on Your Valuables

While visiting Greece, it's crucial to keep a check on your possessions like you would in any location. Keep your wallet, phone, and other valuables in a safe place since pickpocketing may be a problem in crowded tourist locations and on public transportation. A smart suggestion is to refrain from carrying a lot of cash or valuable jewelry.

Here are some pointers to keep your belongings secure when visiting Greece:

Keep your valuables close: While you're out and about, keep your wallet, phone, and other valuables in a safe place, such as a pocket with a zipper or a cross-body bag you can carry in front of you. Do not hold your phone carelessly in your hand or carry your bag on your back.

Be cautious on public transport: Keep a tight check on your valuables while using public transportation since pickpocketing may be an issue on crowded buses and trains. Avoid lugging around a bulky suitcase or backpack that someone behind you may readily open.

Avoid leaving valuables in your hotel room: Although hotel rooms in Greece are often secure, it is still advisable to keep your belongings close to you when you are out and about. Use the hotel safe or lock up your belongings in your bag if you must leave valuables in your room.

Don't leave bags unattended: Keep your luggage close to you at all times while you're out and about at a café or restaurant. Do not even briefly leave it alone since this might make it a target for theft.

Avoid wearing expensive jewelry: When on vacation, it may be tempting to flaunt your finest jewelry, but it is preferable to leave pricey pieces at home. You may become a target as a result, particularly in busy places.

Don't carry large amounts of cash: Carrying just the amount of cash you will need for the day and putting the remainder in a hotel safe or another secure location is a smart idea. If you must use an ATM, be sure to do it in a well-lit, secure location.

It's wise to take precautions with your belongings wherever you travel, and Greece is no different. Despite Greece's generally low crime rate, theft, and pickpocketing may nevertheless happen in popular tourist sites, particularly during the summer.

Be Aware of Your Surroundings

Always be alert of your surroundings while you're out and about. This entails being vigilant and aware of the people, places, and things around you. Avoid going alone in locations with poor lighting, and exercise caution if somebody attempts to talk to you or otherwise divert your attention.

The key to remaining safe when traveling, particularly in foreign settings, is to be alert to your surroundings. Like in any area, travelers who are not mindful of their surroundings may fall prey to scams, theft, or other risks in Greece. Here are some pointers to help you be vigilant and minimize risks:

Stay Alert: Always be aware of your surroundings, particularly in busy places like marketplaces, tourist attractions, and public transit. Try to keep your valuables near your body and avoid leaving them unattended if you are in a busy environment. Also, it's a good idea to be aware of any emergency exits or escape routes.

Be Cautious: Be wary if someone attempts to talk to you or else divert your attention. Despite the fact that most residents are kind and helpful, some may attempt to con or steal from visitors. Trust your instincts and leave a situation if you feel uneasy or uncertain about it.

Avoid Walking Alone: Everywhere you go, walking alone may be perilous, particularly at night. If you must go alone, stay in well-lit areas and steer clear of taking detours via lonely or silent neighborhoods. In case of an emergency, it's a good idea to have a personal alarm or whistle with you.

Stay Informed: It's a good idea to learn about Greek traditions and legislation before your trip. It might be easier to prevent misunderstandings and cultural gaffes if you know what to anticipate. Moreover, you should look for any travel warnings or advisories that have been issued by your government or local authorities.

Trust Your Instincts: Trust your instincts and leave a situation if you feel uneasy or uncertain about it. Never feel compelled to do anything you don't want to do, and never be embarrassed to ask for assistance if you do. Always put your safety first and remember that it's better to be safe than sorry.

You can contribute to ensuring a secure and pleasurable vacation to Greece by being aware of your surroundings, being vigilant, and according to these suggestions. No place is completely risk-free, but by taking the required safety measures and maintaining knowledge, you can remain safe and have a worry-free trip.

Use Reputable Taxis

Although using trustworthy businesses may help to protect your safety, taxis can be an easy way to move about Greece. Avoid hailing cabs on the street since they could not be licensed and can be harmful. Instead, use a ride-sharing app like Uber or Bolt, or ask your hotel or restaurant to make a cab call on your behalf.

Hiring trustworthy cabs is crucial safety advice for tourists to Greece. Although Greek cabs are often trustworthy and safe, there are some dishonest drivers who can attempt to take advantage of visitors. The following advice is for utilizing taxis in Greece:

Use licensed taxis: Greece requires licensed taxis to have a taxi meter and a yellow and black checkered symbol on the top of the vehicle. Taxis lacking these indicators should be avoided since they could not have a license.

Ask for the price before you get in: When you board the taxi, it's a good idea to ask the driver for an expected fee, particularly for farther distances. By doing this, you may prevent any unforeseen fees or legal issues in the future.

Avoid getting scammed: Some taxi drivers could attempt to rip off travelers by taking longer journeys or charging more than necessary. Make sure the meter is functioning correctly by keeping an eye on it. You may refuse to pay and call the authorities for help if you think the fare is excessive or the driver is being dishonest.

Use ride-sharing apps: An easier and safer way to move about Greece is by using a ride-sharing app like Uber or Bolt. These applications enable you to follow your driver's whereabouts in real time and provide a precise fee estimate.

Have the address written down: It's a good idea to have the address of your destination written down in Greek if you are unfamiliar with the region. This may assist in preventing any misunderstandings or confusion with the driver.

Using reputable taxis and taking precautions against scams can help ensure a safe and hassle-free experience when traveling in Greece.

Practice Safe Driving

It's crucial to use defensive driving techniques if you want to hire a vehicle or scooter in Greece. Greek drivers may be aggressive, and the roads can be congested and twisty. Always buckle up, follow the rules of the road, and drive safely at night in inclement weather.

For visitors who are not acquainted with the local driving customs and laws, driving in Greece might be difficult. Here are some pointers for driving securely in Greece:

Get Familiar with Local Driving Habits: Driving in Greece may not be as familiar to you as it is in your native country. Greek motorists may be aggressive, and they often break traffic laws. To prevent accidents, it's critical to pay attention to and adjust to the driving styles of other cars.

Rent a Car from a Reputable Agency: Choose a trustworthy company that provides adequate insurance coverage and dependable automobiles by doing some research before renting a car. Whether you want to drive in the city or off-road, it's essential to choose a vehicle that is appropriate for the sort of driving you'll be doing.

Always Wear a Seatbelt: In Greece, both the driver and every passenger are required to use a seatbelt. Be sure the seatbelts in your rental vehicle are in good functioning order and always wear them.

Follow Traffic Rules: Driving is done on the right side of the road in Greece, and the right is given preference. Keep to the right at all times, stop at all red lights, and give way to pedestrians. The penalties for exceeding stated speed restrictions are severe.

Be Cautious on Narrow Roads: Many of the roads in Greece are curvy, small, and without guardrails. On these routes, use caution and refrain from overtaking unless you can clearly see the road in front of you.

Avoid Driving at Night: The lighting on Greek roads may be weak, making it more difficult to see other cars, people walking, and objects at night. If you must drive at night, turn on your headlights and drive carefully.

Watch out for Animals: Animals like lambs and goats that may stray into the road in Greece are a common sight. Driving in rural regions requires additional caution; keep an eye out for animals near the road or on it.

Plan Ahead: If you want to go a great distance by car, be careful to map out your route in advance and schedule rest stops and stretching sessions. To prevent getting lost, it's also a good idea to have a GPS or map.

You may assure a safe and pleasurable driving experience in Greece by paying attention to these pointers. There are alternative ways to get about if you don't feel comfortable driving, such as using public transit or hiring a driver.

Stay Hydrated

Keep in mind that Greece has hot, muggy summers, and drink plenty of water. While spending time outside, particularly in the heat of the day, be sure you drink enough water and rest up.

While vacationing in Greece, especially during the summer, staying hydrated is essential for good health and preventing heat-related ailments. Greece has a Mediterranean climate, with hot, dry summers and warm, rainy winters. The months of July and August are exceptionally hot, with daily highs in certain regions topping 40°C (104°F) and often exceeding 30°C (86°F).

Drink lots of water throughout the day to keep hydrated, particularly if you're spending time outside. Carrying a reusable water bottle is a smart idea, and you can fill it up at one of the many public water fountains or faucets present in most towns and cities. Customers may also get free glasses of water in a lot of cafés and eateries.

Fruit juices, coconut water, and herbal teas are additional hydrating choices to water. Nonetheless, it's crucial to be aware of the sugar level in certain beverages and to stay away from anything that contains these ingredients since they might cause dehydration.

It's also crucial to avoid overworking oneself between 11:00 am and 4:00 pm when it's usually the warmest of the day. At this period, if you want to engage in any outside activity, remember to often rest in the shade and drink plenty of water.

Dehydration may cause headaches, weariness, dry mouth, and vertigo. It's crucial to stop what you're doing and relax in a cool, shaded spot if you suffer any of these symptoms. Up till you feel better, think about taking a break from outside activities and drinking plenty of water or other hydrating liquids.

In addition to drinking enough water, you should shield your skin from the sun's UV rays. Use a broad-spectrum sunscreen every two hours, or more often if you're swimming or perspiring, with an SPF of at least 30. To protect your face and eyes, put on a wide-brimmed hat and sunglasses. You may also want to consider wearing breathable, light clothes made of natural materials like cotton or linen.

In conclusion, it is essential to keep hydrated when vacationing in Greece in order to preserve excellent health and prevent heat-related ailments. Be sure to stay hydrated all day, refrain from straining yourself too much while it's hot outside, and use sunscreen to shield yourself from the sun's dangerous UV rays. You can take advantage of all Greece has to offer while being safe and healthy by adhering to these easy suggestions.

Be Prepared for Emergency Situations

Although it's rare that an emergency would arise while you're vacationing in Greece, it's always a good idea to be ready. Be certain you know how to reach your embassy or consulate as well as the neighborhood emergency services. To cover unforeseen medical costs or trip delays, think about getting travel insurance.

It's crucial to be ready for emergencies in any vacation location, and Greece is no different. While a significant emergency won't likely arise while you're vacationing in Greece, it's always a good idea to be ready just in case. Here are some pointers to help you be ready for emergencies when visiting Greece.

Understand how to contact your embassy or consulate

In the event of an emergency, it's critical to have access to your embassy's or consulate's contact details. From lost or stolen passports to urgent medical situations, your embassy or consulate may provide support. Have your embassy or consulate's contact details with you at all times by writing them down.

Know the Local Emergency Services

Knowing how to reach the local emergency services is crucial in the event of a catastrophic emergency. The emergency number in Greece is 112. This number may be used in case of fire, police, or medical emergencies. Have the emergency number with you at all times by writing it down.

Consider Purchasing Travel Insurance

To cover unforeseen medical costs or travel delays, travel insurance might be a wise investment. Knowing that you are protected in case of emergency may also be reassuring. Have a copy of your policy on hand, along with your contact information, and thoroughly study the policy to understand what is and isn't covered.

Be Prepared for Natural Disasters

Natural catastrophes like earthquakes and wildfires are common in Greece. Even if these occurrences are uncommon, it's crucial to be ready just in case. Learn the emergency evacuation procedure if you are staying in a hotel. Be careful to locate earthquake-safe locations if you're staying on private property. Water, non-perishable food, and any required prescriptions should always be available.

Know Your Health Needs

Be sure to pack adequate medicine for the length of your vacation if you have any pre-existing medical issues. If you need medical care while visiting Greece, be warned that it may not be like what you're accustomed to. Before leaving home, it's a good idea to investigate healthcare facilities and providers. You should also have a plan in place in case of a medical emergency.

You may take pleasure in a risk-free and stress-free journey to Greece by being aware of the possible hazards and planning for emergency scenarios. Keep in mind to be vigilant and aware of your surroundings at all times, as well as to carry crucial papers and contact information with you. By taking these safety measures, you may enjoy Greece's natural beauty and rich culture without having to worry about your safety.

Respect Local Customs and Laws

Lastly, while visiting Greece, it's crucial to observe regional laws and traditions. While visiting holy places, dress modestly, abstain from public shows of love, and be knowledgeable of regional traditions. Greek law has strict penalties for using drugs, alcohol, or other substances, therefore it's necessary to be informed of them.

Traveling responsibly and safely in Greece necessitates respecting regional laws and traditions. Despite the fact that Greece is a generally hospitable and kind nation, it's crucial to respect local customs and traditions. Observe the following advice:

Dress Appropriately: Greece is a conservative nation, therefore it's vital to wear modest clothing, especially while visiting places of worship. This entails protecting your knees and shoulders as well as staying away from tight or exposing attire.

Respect Religious Sites: Many historic and significant religious structures, such as monasteries, cathedrals, and temples, may be found throughout Greece. It's vital to respect these locations when you visit them by remaining silent, not taking photographs (if it's forbidden), and according to any other regulations or instructions.

Avoid Public Displays of Affection: Greeks tend to avoid showing their devotion in front of others. Although modest affection or hand-holding are often appropriate, more overt shows of closeness should be avoided.

Be Mindful of Traditions: Particularly in smaller towns and villages, Greece is home to a wide variety of distinctive traditions and customs. Whether it's a regional celebration or a traditional feast, be accepting and appreciative of these customs.

Know the Laws: Greece has its own laws and rules, just like any other nation. Particularly when it comes to drugs, alcohol, and other substances, it's critical to be aware of them. Because of the potential severity of the penalties for breaching these rules, it is crucial to use prudence and good judgment.

If you take the appropriate safety measures, traveling in Greece can be a safe and pleasurable experience. You may assist to guarantee trouble-free travel by keeping a watch on your possessions, being mindful of your surroundings, and obeying local traditions and laws.

Scams and Crime to Watch Out for in Greece

Greece has a low rate of violent crime, making it a somewhat safe destination for travelers. Travelers should be careful of possible frauds and small-time crime, however, as in any place. There are several frauds and crimes in Greece that you should be aware of.

Fake police scams

The "fake police" fraud is among the most prevalent in Greece. A con artist will stop visitors and demand to see their passports and wallets while posing as a police officer. They could ask to inspect the person's possessions and claim to be hunting for narcotics, counterfeit money, or stolen goods. The perpetrator will either take the victim's wallet or give it back while saying that some of the cash or papers are fraudulent and need to be seized. Always request identification, and if you have any worries, get in touch with the neighborhood police station to avoid falling for this swindle.

Criminals often employ the "fake police" scam to take advantage of ignorant visitors in Greece. Even though this kind of fraud may occur everywhere, it's crucial to be informed of the particulars of this fraud in Greece in order to prevent being a victim.

The con usually starts with a person approaching visitors on the street while posing as a police officer. They could even display a badge or identity card to give the impression that they are a real law enforcement official while wearing a convincing police outfit. They may then demand to view the tourist's passport and pocketbook while making excuses about searching for stolen goods, counterfeit currency, or narcotics.

After a quick inspection of the victim's wallet, the con artist may hand it back while stating that some of the cash or papers are phony and need to be seized. As an alternative, they may just take the victim's wallet and vanish.

There are a few important considerations to make in order to prevent being a victim of this fraud. When contacted by someone claiming to be a police officer, always demand identification. Any inquiries you may have will be answered and their credentials will be proudly shown by legitimate police officers. Contact your neighborhood police station and seek advice if you have any questions.

Keeping your wallet and other valuables in a secret pocket or other safe area is also a smart idea. Keep your cash to a minimum, and never leave your possessions unattended.

The "tourist tax" fraud is another scam that is prevalent in Greece. This con involves approaching visitors and telling them that they must pay a certain tax or charge in order to visit a specific location or destination. They can demand a big amount or demand payment in a strange currency. In fact, there is no such tax or charge, and the individual is only attempting to take advantage of visitors who are not paying attention.

It's crucial to conduct your homework before visiting any places or attractions to prevent falling for this scam. To obtain an idea of what the entry prices should be, consult the official websites and guidebooks. Be suspicious of anybody who requests payment in an abnormally big amount of money or in a currency that isn't widely accepted.

It's critical to remain alert to the theft of all kinds, especially pickpocketing, in popular tourist places. Be wary of anybody who attempts to talk to you or distract you, and keep your possessions close to your body. Avoid carrying a lot of cash, and use ATMs with caution.

Greece is a secure place to visit, but in order to keep safe and protect your things, you need to be aware of any possible scams and crimes. You may take advantage of all Greece has to offer without being a victim of fraud or crime by exercising care, completing your homework, and using common sense safety measures.

Pickpocketing and theft

On public transportation and in crowded tourist places, pickpocketing may be a concern. Thieves sometimes operate in gangs and use noise-making devices or other methods to deflect attention while they take valuables like wallets, phones, and other items. Keep your possessions safe and near to your body, as in a money belt or crossbody bag, to prevent pickpocketing. Avoid wearing pricey jewelry or carrying a lot of cash.

In Greece, stealing and pickpocketing are frequent crimes, especially in busy tourist locations and on public transportation.

Thieves sometimes operate in gangs and use a variety of strategies, such as bumping into their targets or creating a ruckus, to divert them. When they pickpocket unwary visitors, they could also divert attention by soliciting directions, offering to buy trinkets, or engaging in street performances.

You may take a number of steps to protect yourself against theft and pickpocketing. Start by always keeping your possessions near to your body and avoiding leaving them unattended in public areas. Choose a purse that is challenging for criminals to reach without your notice, such as a crossbody bag or money belt. It's also a good idea to leave any superfluous items, such as pricey jewelry, at home and only carry tiny quantities of cash.

Keep an eye on your possessions and use additional caution while taking public transit. Refrain from flaunting pricey stuff like cellphones or cameras in public since doing so might make you a target for theft. Avoid standing close to the doors of trains or buses if you must use your phone, and keep it in your pocket or bag while not in use.

Be watchful and mindful of your surroundings while you're in busy places like marketplaces and shopping malls. Avoid putting your wallet in your back pocket and keep your bag closed with the zipper facing front. Keep your money in a front pocket or a safe place since thieves may readily take it from your rear pockets.

If you do become a victim of theft, notify the authorities in your area right away. Take a snapshot of your passport and any credit cards you are carrying, and keep a duplicate of it and any critical papers in a secure location. This will make it easier for you to alert the authorities right away if something is missing or has been stolen.

It's crucial to remember that not all Greeks steal or pickpocket; in fact, the great majority are trustworthy and kind toward visitors. To prevent being a victim of crime, it is essential to constantly be cautious and vigilant. You may have peace of mind when visiting Greece if you safeguard your possessions and pay attention to your surroundings.

Fake vendors and products

In Greece, tourists could run across street hawkers peddling phony designer handbags and sunglasses. Some sellers could also use high-pressure sales techniques or claim that the goods are genuine. Get goods from reliable retailers or sellers, and always verify the product's quality before making a purchase, to avoid falling for this con.

The selling of false or counterfeit goods is another typical fraud in Greece. Vendors peddling replica designer handbags, sunglasses, and jewelry may easily con tourists. These sellers often use high-pressure sales techniques or claim that the goods are genuine, but in practice, the goods are of low quality and not worth the money.

It's crucial to get things from reliable stores or merchants to prevent falling for this con. Stay with well-known brands and refrain from buying anything that seems too good to be true since it's probably real. Also, before making a purchase, always confirm the product's quality. Look closely for any evidence of wear and tear, such as frayed threads or subpar materials.

The unique rules governing the purchasing of products in Greece must also be understood. For instance, purchasing or selling counterfeit goods is prohibited, and travelers who are discovered doing so risk paying hefty penalties or possibly going to jail. Also, it's against the law and may have severe legal repercussions to buy things like ivory or other endangered animals.

Always err on the side of caution and refrain from making a purchase if you have any doubts about the legitimacy of a product or the legality of a transaction. Avoid buying things from unregistered dealers or street vendors and only purchase at trustworthy establishments.

Visitors visiting Greece should be alert of other thefts, such as hotel room theft and bag snatching, in addition to these typical con games. Always keep your valuables locked up and avoid leaving them unattended in public places to prevent theft. Avoid carrying large sums of cash or wearing pricey jewelry, and instead use hotel safes or lockboxes to hold your passport, cash, and other critical papers.

Keep a copy of your passport and other critical papers in case they become lost or stolen, along with a list of emergency phone contacts. This may assist you in reporting the incident to local law enforcement promptly and efficiently and in taking action to avoid identity theft or other sorts of fraud.

Greece is a relatively secure place to visit, but you should be aware of frequent scams and take precautions to keep yourself safe from theft and other forms of crime. You may assist guarantee a safe and pleasurable journey to this beautiful nation by paying attention to these suggestions and being attentive and aware of your surroundings.

Restaurant and bar scams

Restaurants and bars may attempt to con visitors in certain tourist destinations by overcharging for food and drink, tacking on extra fees, or adopting a "bait-and-switch" scheme. Check pricing before placing an order, request an itemized statement, and be aware of any additional fees to avoid falling for this con. Reading reviews of restaurants and bars before going there is also a smart idea.

In tourist destinations of Greece, restaurant and bar scams may be an issue, thus it's essential for visitors to be aware of the strategies utilized by dishonest business owners. Overcharging for meals and drinks is one prevalent fraud. This may take many different forms, such as increasing rates for visitors or tacking on more fees without providing a justification. It's a good idea to verify pricing before placing an order and to request an itemized statement that details the cost of each item to prevent falling for this con.

Several pubs and restaurants also use the bait-and-switch strategy. This scam involves a company advertising a cheap price for a drink or meal, but when the consumer shows up there, they are informed that the advertised item is either unavailable or only available at a significantly higher price. Read restaurant and bar reviews before going, and be skeptical of any establishment that looks to be giving offers that seem too good to be true in order to avoid falling for this scam.

The "tourist menu" is a typical restaurant and bar scam. There may be things on this menu that are not generally included on the regular menu since it is expressly created to appeal to travelers. Yet, compared to the standard menu choices, these dishes are often more expensive and of inferior quality. It's a good idea to request the standard menu and to refrain from ordering anything that isn't on it in order to avoid falling for this con.

Travelers should be careful of establishments that automatically add a gratuity or service fee to the bill in addition to these frauds. Although leaving a tip is typical in Greece, it's a good idea to know what to anticipate before going to a restaurant. Moreover, it's a good idea to keep little notes and change on hand since some establishments can say they don't have change for bigger amounts.

It's a good idea to study establishments before coming, to ask for suggestions from locals or other visitors, and to be aware of establishments that appear unduly aggressive or forceful in order to avoid falling for restaurant and bar scams. Also, it's critical to believe your gut and be prepared to leave if something doesn't seem right.

Scams in restaurants and bars are not frequent in Greece's tourist locations, but they may be avoided with a little bit of study and care. You can take advantage of everything that Greece has to offer without falling prey to dishonest company owners by being aware of these scams and taking precautions to protect yourself.

Taxi scams

In Greece, some taxi drivers may attempt to overcharge tourists, take longer routes to raise the fee, or make meter-related excuses. Choose trustworthy taxi companies or request that your hotel or restaurant contact a cab for you to avoid falling for this con. Moreover, you may utilize ride-sharing services like Uber or Bolt.

In many places in Greece, particularly in tourist destinations, taxi scams may be an issue. While taking cabs, it's important to be aware of any possible hazards and take precautions to keep yourself safe.

Overcharging, when the driver charges more than the metered rate or adds on extra expenses, is a typical taxi fraud. Make sure you are aware of the fee before boarding the cab in order to avoid falling for this scam. If at all possible, get a rough sense of the fare from the locals or the employees at your hotel so you know what to anticipate. Before getting in the vehicle, you may alternatively ask the driver to start the meter or negotiate a fare.

Taking longer routes in order to charge more for a cab is another taxi scam. Some drivers may intentionally get lost or take a detour to increase the fee. Use a map or GPS navigation device to keep track of the trip to prevent this. Speak out and tell the driver to take the shortest path to your destination if you think they are taking a longer route.

In rare circumstances, cabbies could even attempt to haggle a higher charge by saying the meter is faulty. Be sure the meter is on and functioning correctly before getting in the cab to prevent falling for this trick. If the driver insists that the meter is faulty, you have two options: request that they switch on the meter or haggle a fare in advance.

Choose trusted taxi companies or request that your hotel or restaurant contact a cab for you to further safeguard yourself against taxi fraud. Moreover, there are ride-sharing applications like Uber and Bolt that provide up-front pricing and a record of your trip.

Before getting into the car, be sure to verify the app's information on the driver and the vehicle, and make sure the driver has started the trip before you leave.

Despite the fact that taxi scams are an issue in Greece, you may avoid being a victim by adopting a few preventative measures. You may travel in Greece with confidence by being alert, choosing trusted taxi services, and using ride-sharing applications.

ATM skimming

In Greece, theft from ATMs is a prevalent crime, especially in popular tourist regions. To steal card data and PINs, thieves install skimming devices in ATMs. Use ATMs in well-lit, busy places, and cover the keypad while entering your PIN to protect yourself from falling for this con. Checking your bank statements often for any fraudulent purchases is another smart move.

When someone uses an ATM, their debit or credit card information and PIN are stolen. This practice is known as ATM skimming. Skimmers gather the information using covert electronic devices like card readers and webcams, which they then use to make fraudulent transactions or remove money from the victim's account.

In Greece, ATM skimming is a major issue, especially in tourist locations where fraudsters prey on unwary tourists who are unfamiliar with the local ATMs. There are numerous measures you may take to guard against ATM skimming.

Secondly, always utilize ATMs that are placed in well-lit, crowded places, including within banks or busy commercial districts. Avoid utilizing ATMs in remote locations since they are more prone to skimming, such as those by the side of the road.

Second, before using the ATM, look for any evidence of manipulation. Verify that the card reader, keypad, and other components of the device seem normal and have not been changed. Skimming devices may be difficult to see, but some frequent indicators include slack or shaky components, materials or colors that don't match, and pinhole or concealed cameras.

Finally, put your hand over the keyboard to enter your PIN. Skimmers often use minute cameras or overlays to capture a person's PIN, which they then exploit to access an account. You can prevent keypad skimmers from viewing your PIN by covering the keypad.

Third, keep a close eye on any unlawful transactions on your bank statements. Report any questionable activity right away to your bank if you see it.

One of the numerous frauds and crimes to be on the lookout for in Greece is ATM skimming. You may safeguard yourself and have a safe and pleasurable journey to this beautiful nation by being cautious and adopting the required safety measures.

Beach scams

In certain tourist regions, individuals may approach guests and say they are renting beach chairs or umbrellas, only to subsequently demand more money or keep their possessions hostage. Always hire beach chairs and umbrellas from reliable sellers, and be mindful of any additional fees or restrictions, to avoid falling for this swindle.

While visiting Greece, travelers should be careful of beach scams. Visitors may come across people in crowded tourist places who promise to rent beach chairs or umbrellas, only to subsequently demand more payment or keep the tourists' possessions hostage. At first, these people could come off as polite and trustworthy, but after they have the visitors' goods, they can become hostile and demand money.

It's crucial to only hire beach chairs and umbrellas from reliable sellers in order to avoid falling for this con. These suppliers won't charge extra fees or keep customers' possessions hostage; instead, they will have transparent pricing and rental-equipment procedures. Also, visitors should be aware of any additional fees or restrictions that may apply while renting beach equipment. It is a good idea to ask for a receipt or other proof of the rental agreement to avoid any misunderstandings.

The "drinks on the beach" scam is another popular beach scam in Greece. This con involves people approaching beachgoers and offering to sell them beverages for less money than the surrounding beach bars. These beverages could be subpar, diluted, or even drug-spiked. Visitors should only buy beverages from respectable beach bars and restaurants to avoid falling for this con.

It's also crucial to exercise caution with strangers on the beach. Tourists who are preoccupied or sleeping on the beach may be the target of thieves who take their things. Tourists should store their valuables in a safe place, such as a hotel safe or a beach bag kept close to their body. Traveling with a friend or family member who can assist keep an eye on items is also a smart option.

Visitors should be mindful of basic safety issues while visiting Greece in addition to these particular scams. Always keep a watch on your personal possessions, particularly while using public transit or in busy settings. Visitors should also be wary of anybody who attempts to talk to them or otherwise diverts their attention, since this may be a pickpocket or other criminal's trick.

Visitors may have a great time in Greece without becoming a victim of fraud or theft by being cautious and remaining alert. It's critical to believe your intuition and exercise caution in any circumstance that looks unreal or unsettling. Immediately notify the local authorities if you are the victim of fraud or other crimes.

Tourists may have a safe and happy journey to Greece by being vigilant and adopting safety measures. Being watchful and on the lookout for possible frauds or crimes is always a good idea, but it's crucial to avoid letting anxiety spoil your trip.

Health and Medical Care in Greece

Greece is a well-liked vacation spot renowned for its breathtaking natural beauty, extensive history, and delectable food. While it is typically a safe place to go to, tourists should be informed of their alternatives for health and medical treatment.

Healthcare System in Greece:

All citizens and permanent residents in Greece have access to a universal healthcare system. A mix of government taxes and social insurance payments is used to support the healthcare system. Healthcare services for citizens and permanent residents are provided by the National Health System (ESY). Visitors visiting Greece are also entitled to emergency medical care, albeit certain procedures may require payment upfront.

Greece's public hospitals, clinics, and health facilities make up the National Health System (ESY), which offers a variety of medical services, including general care, specialized treatment, and emergency services. The Social Security Institute (IKA) affiliation or paying out-of-pocket for private healthcare services are two ways that patients might acquire healthcare services.

General practitioners and family physicians are the initial point of contact for people seeking medical treatment in Greece and offer primary care services. In their neighborhood health center, which is often staffed by a group of physicians, nurses, and other healthcare workers, patients may schedule appointments to visit a doctor. Health centers provide general care as well as preventative care services including immunizations and tests for diseases.

Greece has hospitals and clinics that provide specialty care services. These facilities are staffed by doctors that specialize in a variety of medical specialties, including cardiology, neurology, and cancer. By a referral from their regular care physician or by going to a private hospital or clinic, patients may get specialist care services.

Greece's National Emergency Ambulance Service (EKAB), which is open twenty-four hours a day, seven days a week, offers emergency medical services. Dial the emergency number 112 in Europe to reach the service. To hospitals and other medical institutions around Greece, EKAB offers emergency medical transport services.

Greece also has private healthcare options, and people may choose between using their own money or private health insurance to obtain these treatments. Specialty care and elective procedures are among the many medical services provided by private hospitals and clinics. The quality of private healthcare services in Greece is typically quite excellent, despite the fact that they might be more costly than those provided by the government.

With highly skilled medical staff and up-to-date facilities, the Greek healthcare system is usually regarded as being of a high caliber. Budget constraints, however, have recently had an impact on the system, causing a lack of medical supplies and higher wait times for certain treatments. Individuals traveling to Greece should make sure they have sufficient travel health insurance to cover any potential medical costs.

Medical Care for Visitors:

It's crucial to get travel health insurance that covers medical costs and emergency evacuation if you're a traveler to Greece. Greek healthcare may be expensive, and certain hospitals could demand advance payment. Having travel health insurance might provide you peace of mind and financial security in the event that you have unanticipated medical problems.

Visitors visiting Greece have the right to emergency medical care, but it's vital to be aware that costs might be costly, particularly for non-urgent or non-emergency procedures. This is why purchasing travel health insurance before visiting Greece is strongly advised. Travel health insurance may cover medical costs, urgent treatment, and even medical evacuation in the event that a tourist has to be sent to a hospital in another city.

It's also crucial to be aware that certain Greek medical institutions could demand payment in advance, particularly for non-emergency medical care. Visitors should be ready to cover the cost of medical treatment out-of-pocket and then submit a claim for reimbursement to their travel health insurance company. Also, travelers should be aware that Greek medical institutions may follow different norms and protocols than those in their own country.

Visitors to Greece should look into the healthcare systems available there before their trip. Also, it's crucial to bring any essential prescription drugs as well as any possible over-the-counter needs. Also, it is advised to include a first aid kit with bandages, antiseptic, and painkillers.

Visitors should use the European Emergency Number 112 for urgent help in case of a medical emergency. To call for an ambulance or other emergency medical help, dial this number. Visitors need to be ready to identify themselves, their location, and the nature of their medical emergency.

Visitors visiting Greece have access to both emergency and non-emergency medical care at governmental and private medical institutions. While public healthcare facilities are sometimes less costly than private healthcare facilities, they can have longer wait periods and worse quality of service. Private hospitals are often more costly yet provide better treatment and quicker service.

Greek healthcare is generally regarded as of high quality, and many of the medical staff members are fluent in English. When in Greece, travelers should nonetheless use care and take precautions to protect their own health and safety. This entails taking precautions against being sick, such as maintaining excellent cleanliness, using bottled water, and avoiding eating raw or undercooked food.

Travelers visiting Greece should get travel health insurance, look into the local healthcare systems, and be ready to foot the bill for any necessary medical treatment. They should also know how to use emergency number 112 in Europe and take precautions against becoming sick while in Greece. Visitors may assist make sure they get the medical treatment they need while in Greece by following these instructions.

Hospitals and Medical Facilities:

Greece has a comprehensive medical infrastructure, including several hospitals, clinics, and treatment centers. In addition to private hospitals and clinics in major cities, public hospitals are spread out over the nation. Greek medical personnel generally provide high-quality treatment, and many of them are fluent in English.

In Greece, public hospitals are typically run by the National Health System and provide citizens and long-term residents with free or inexpensive medical care. These government-funded hospitals provide critical medical services including emergency treatment, surgery, and outpatient care. They often have up-to-date medical technology and highly skilled medical personnel working for them.

Greece also has private hospitals and clinics, which provide a larger variety of medical services than state hospitals. They often provide more specialized treatment and lower wait times. Compared to public hospitals, private medical facilities often have higher prices and demand upfront payment or payment via travel health insurance.

In Greece, general practitioners and medical specialists are often in charge of providing medical treatment. Medical specialists are practitioners who specialize in certain medical specialties, such as cardiology or oncology, whereas general practitioners are primary care physicians who provide normal medical treatment.

Greek medical workers are educated to worldwide standards, and the majority of hospitals and medical institutions are outfitted with cutting-edge medical technology. Many medical staff, including physicians, speak English, and some hospitals may provide translation services for clients who don't understand Greek.

Greece has a large number of pharmacies that sell both prescription and over-the-counter medicines. Pharmacists are highly qualified medical specialists who may provide medical advice and recommendations for over-the-counter drugs. Several pharmacies are open twenty-four hours a day.

The national emergency number in Greece in case of a medical emergency is 112. You may call this number to get in touch with the police, fire department, and emergency medical services. Modern medical technology and highly skilled medical personnel are both found in Greek ambulances.

Greece has a comprehensive medical infrastructure, including several hospitals, clinics, and treatment centers. Greece offers high-quality healthcare, and many physicians and other medical personnel are fluent in English. Visitors should be aware of the possible costs of medical treatment in Greece and should carry travel health insurance to cover medical bills and emergency evacuation.

Pharmacies:

Greece has several readily accessible pharmacies that may provide guidance and simple medical treatment. In Greece, many drugs that need a prescription in other nations may be bought without one. It's crucial to keep in mind that drug availability might vary by area and that certain drugs could not be accessible without a prescription.

Greek pharmacies, or "Farmakeio," are commonplace and may be found in almost every neighborhood and city. They are crucial in giving Greek citizens basic medical treatment and guidance. Greece has strong restrictions controlling the functioning of pharmacies, which are privately held. The National Organization of Medicines (EOF), which is in charge of ensuring that all pharmacies adhere to the stringent rules on medication dispensation, grants licenses to pharmacies.

Greek pharmacies provide both prescription and non-prescription drugs. In Greece, many drugs that need a prescription in other nations may be bought without one. Antibiotics, anti-inflammatory meds, and other medications for chronic diseases fall under this category. However, in Greece, several drugs that are sold over the counter in other nations could need a prescription. It is important to remember that drug availability may differ depending on region, and certain drugs could not be accessible without a prescription.

Greek pharmacists have extensive training and a deep understanding of drugs and how they interact. Moreover, they are competent to provide basic medical guidance and may suggest over-the-counter drugs for conditions like colds and allergies. Greek pharmacies are expected to speak fluent English, making it simpler for visitors and expats to converse with them.

It's vital to keep in mind that most Greek pharmacies follow a rotating schedule. As a result, not every pharmacy is open at the same time. There is a duty pharmacy in each area that is open beyond normal business hours. Every pharmacy's entrance has information about where the duty pharmacy is located.

Medication costs in Greece are often lower than in many other nations. It is crucial to remember that the cost of prescriptions might vary based on the brand, the kind of medication, and the pharmacy's location. For certain categories of individuals, including students, retirees, and those with chronic diseases, several pharmacies in Greece provide discounts on medicine.

Greek pharmacies are crucial to the country's healthcare system since they make prescriptions and simple medical advice readily available. Travelers visiting Greece should be aware that drug availability varies by region and that certain drugs may not be accessible without a prescription. Particularly for people with chronic ailments or those who are traveling for a lengthy amount of time, it is important to obtain travel health insurance that pays for medical costs and emergency evacuation.

Emergency Medical Care:

Visitors visiting Greece may use the country's emergency number, which is 112 in case of a medical emergency. Greece's emergency services are often effective, and ambulance response times are frequently quick. It's crucial to remember that visitors may have to pay out of pocket for emergency medical treatment since ambulance services are not free.

Visitors visiting Greece may use the country's emergency number, which is 112 in case of a medical emergency. The 112 emergency number is accessible around-the-clock from any phone, including payphones and mobile devices. Ambulances, firemen, and police are just a few of the emergency services that the operator will be able to summon as needed.

Greece's emergency medical services are often effective, and ambulance response times are frequently quick. The medical staff on board ambulances is trained to provide first medical treatment while the patient is being transported to the hospital, and ambulances are equipped with basic life support equipment. It's crucial to remember that visitors may have to pay out of pocket for emergency medical treatment since ambulance services are not free. To find out whether their travel insurance coverage covers emergency medical treatment, customers should verify with their provider.

Knowing where the closest hospital or medical institution is in Greece is crucial if you ever need emergency medical attention. Hospitals and other medical facilities are widely dispersed throughout the nation. In most large cities, there are both public hospitals and private hospitals and clinics. Greece offers typically high-quality healthcare, and many physicians and other medical personnel are fluent in English.

Bring your passport or a copy of your passport, as well as the details of your travel insurance, if you need to attend a hospital or medical institution in Greece. Visitors should be prepared to pay for medical treatments out of pocket if required since certain hospitals may ask for upfront payment. Moreover, it's a good idea to include any medical documents or paperwork that the treating physician would find useful, a list of any drugs you are presently taking, and other pertinent information.

Greece has several readily accessible pharmacies that may provide guidance and simple medical treatment. In Greece, many drugs that need a prescription in other nations may be bought without one. It's crucial to keep in mind that drug availability might vary by area and that certain drugs could not be accessible without a prescription. Before buying any drugs, guests should consult with a pharmacist or medical expert to make sure they are secure and suitable for their requirements.

Greece's emergency medical services are often effective, and ambulance response times are frequently quick. Visitors should be informed that emergency medical treatment may require them to make their own personal payments since ambulance services are not always free. Greece has a large number of hospitals and healthcare facilities spread out over the nation, and the country offers typically high-quality medical treatment. While seeking medical treatment in

Greece, visitors should carry their passports, information about their travel insurance, and any relevant medical papers. Greece's pharmacies are conveniently located and able to provide simple medical assistance and guidance, but travelers should be aware that certain drugs may not be accessible without a prescription.

Common Health Concerns in Greece:

Greece is generally a safe and healthy country to visit. However, travelers should be aware of some common health concerns, including:

Sunburn and Heat Stroke: Greece has a Mediterranean climate with hot summers and mild winters. It's important to wear sunscreen, stay hydrated, and avoid prolonged exposure to the sun to prevent sunburn and heat stroke.

Food and Water Safety: While Greece has high food safety standards, travelers should be cautious when consuming food and water. It's important to drink bottled or boiled water, avoid ice in drinks, and only consume food that has been cooked thoroughly.

Mosquito-Borne Illnesses: During the summer months, mosquitoes can be a nuisance in some areas of Greece. Mosquito-borne illnesses such as West Nile virus and malaria are rare but can occur. Travelers should take precautions to prevent mosquito bites, such as using insect repellent and wearing long-sleeved clothing.

Allergies: Greece is home to a variety of plants and trees that can cause allergies in some people. If you have allergies, it's important to bring any necessary medications with you and to be aware of the potential triggers.

With a cutting-edge healthcare system and a wide range of medical facilities, Greece is a safe and healthy holiday destination. Travelers should take preventative measures to safeguard their health, such as applying sunscreen, getting travel health insurance, and being cautious with their food and drink. Travelers may take advantage of everything that Greece has to offer while being healthy and safe by being organized and knowledgeable.

Part V: Crete

Chapter 12: Discovering Crete

The Best Beaches in Crete

Some of the most gorgeous beaches in the Mediterranean may be found in Crete, the biggest of the Greek islands. The island's beaches are ideal for unwinding, swimming, and soaking up the sun thanks to its crystal-clear seas, breathtaking natural settings, and an assortment of services and activities. These are a few of Crete's top beaches:

Elafonisi Beach

Elafonisi Beach, which is situated on Crete's southwest coast, is renowned for its pink sand and blue waves. The beach is bordered by rare plant species, cedar trees, and sand dunes since it is part of a protected nature reserve. Families with small children will find it to be the perfect location due to the shallow waters and calm waves, while snorkelers may explore the neighboring reef.

Tourists often go to Elafonisi Beach, which is regarded as one of Crete's most stunning beaches. When observed from a distance, the pink sand's distinctive pink hue is the result of minute shell and coral pieces blending with the white sand. The beach's crystal-clear waters are wonderful for swimming and water sports, and its smooth, powdery sand is perfect for sunbathing.

The nearby Elafonisi Island, which is one of the beach's primary attractions, lies only a few meters off the coast. A tiny lagoon that is often just waist-deep separates the island from the mainland. The island's stunning terrain, which is scattered with sand dunes and covered with cedar trees, is accessible by foot by those who want to explore it. Sea lilies and sea daffodils are two uncommon plant species that may be found on the island.

Elafonisi Beach is a great vacation spot for families with small kids since it is safe for them to play and swim in the shallow waters and calm waves. Together with other facilities, the beach is furnished with sun loungers, showers, and dressing rooms. Nearby dining establishments and cafés provide typical Cretan fare, in addition to cool beverages and ice cream.

Elafonisi Beach is a great place for snorkeling aficionados to explore the adjacent reef. Many marine species, such as colorful fish, sea urchins, and starfish, call the reef home. Visitors may rent snorkeling gear from the seaside stores nearby, and they can also schedule a guided snorkeling excursion to explore the reef.

Anybody visiting Crete should be sure to stop at Elafonisi Beach. It is a favored destination for both visitors and residents because of its breathtaking natural beauty, distinctive pink sand, and beautiful seas. Elafonisi Beach offers activities for everyone, whether you wish to swim, sunbathe, or explore the island and its surroundings.

Balos Lagoon

On Crete's northwest coast sits the beautiful natural beauty known as Balos Lagoon. The lagoon is surrounded by craggy hills and high cliffs, with only a little strip of sand separating it from the ocean. Swimming is a breeze in the shallow waters, and lounging and sunbathing are beautiful against the picturesque background of the limestone cliffs. From the adjacent settlement of Kaliviani, the lagoon is accessible by boat or on foot.

Balos Lagoon is a remarkable natural landmark that attracts tourists with its crystal-clear turquoise waters and breathtaking vistas. The lagoon is situated on Crete's northwest coast, halfway between the island of Tigani and the Cape of Gramvousa. The lagoon is a shallow and tranquil swimming area since the sea is isolated from it by a short strip of sand.

The lagoon's waters are very clean, making them perfect for swimming and snorkeling since many fish and other marine life can be seen below the surface. The cliffs and hills that surround the lagoon may be seen in spectacular detail when visitors explore the region by boat. The trip takes approximately an hour, and the boats normally leave from Kissamos or the port of Gramvousa.

Visitors may trek from the adjacent town of Kaliviani to Balos Lagoon in addition to swimming and snorkeling there. The trek is roughly 8 kilometers long and lasts for about two hours, but it is well worth the effort because of the breathtaking landscape along the route. A well-marked path leads hikers over rocky hills and valleys with beautiful views of the sea and coastline.

The grand Venetian fortification of Gramvousa, which is perched on a rocky island in the midst of the lagoon, is one of the attractions of Balos Lagoon. The fortification was constructed in the sixteenth century to protect the island from invaders and pirates. Visitors to the stronghold may take a boat excursion there to see the remains and take in the breathtaking views of the lagoon.

Many animals and plant species, including uncommon birds, reptiles, and plant species, may be found in the vicinity of Balos Lagoon. To understand more about the region's history, vegetation, and animals, tourists may join guided tours of the area.

A must-see spot for anybody visiting Crete is Balos Lagoon. Its gorgeous surroundings, crystal clear waterways, and rich history make it a really unique and remarkable experience. You will undoubtedly be amazed by the breathtaking natural splendor of this wonderful place whether you decide to walk, swim, or take a boat trip.

Falassarna Beach

Falassarna Beach is a wide expanse of golden sand that spans many kilometers along the western coast of Crete. Although the high winds and waves near the northern end of the beach are perfect for windsurfing and kitesurfing, the beautiful, turquoise seas and calm waves make it an excellent place for swimming. Together with various beach bars and eateries, the beach is also home to a tiny historic port.

One of the busiest beaches on Crete's western coast is Falassarna Beach. It is the perfect location for swimming and tanning due to its extensive stretch of golden sand, clean seas, and calm waves. The beach is situated near the town of Falassarna of the same name, which is approximately 12 kilometers from Kissamos and 60 kilometers from Chania.

There are various distinct portions of Falassarna Beach, each with its own distinctive characteristics. Strong winds and big waves at the beach's northern end make it a well-liked location for windsurfing and kitesurfing. The broadest and busiest section of the beach is in the middle, where you may rent beach chairs and umbrellas. The beach is calmer and less busy on the southern end, and there are more isolated areas for swimming and tanning.

Falassarna Beach's crystal-clear seas, which provide exceptional visibility for scuba diving and snorkeling, are one of its most noteworthy qualities. Exploring the undersea realm allows visitors to see a variety of marine life, such as colorful fish, octopuses, and sea urchins. Moreover, tourists may still see the ruins of the harbor walls near the shore, which is where a little old port from the Hellenistic era once stood.

Falassarna Beach is the ideal location for nature enthusiasts since it is surrounded by beautiful hills. Explore the neighboring paths and take in the breathtaking views of the sea and the surroundings.

Thyme, sage, and oregano are just a few of the Mediterranean plants and herbs that blanket the hills, giving them a fragrant smell.

The beach is also home to a number of beach bars and eateries that provide a selection of foods and beverages. Traditional Greek fare, fresh fish, and cool beverages are available for visitors to sample while admiring the sea. Evenings at the beach taverns and eateries are particularly busy since live music and other entertainment are sometimes offered.

Anybody visiting Crete should be sure to stop at Falassarna Beach. It is the ideal location for swimming, sunbathing, and water sports because of its long stretch of golden beach, clean seas, and calm waves. It's a terrific area to unwind and take in the natural beauty of Crete because of its picturesque surroundings, historic port, and an assortment of beach bars and restaurants.

Vai Beach

On Crete's northeastern coast, Vai Beach is distinguished by a lovely palm grove. The island's natural palm trees surround the sandy beach in a thick forest, and the crystal-clear waters are ideal for swimming and snorkeling. There are several pubs and cafés close by, and the beach is accessible by vehicle or boat.

On the Greek island of Crete's northeastern shore, Vai Beach is a remote gem. The beach is well-known for having a genuine palm grove, which is unusual and uncommon in Europe. Date seeds left behind by Arab pirates who pillaged the island in the ninth century are said to be the source of the palm grove. s a

Around 200 meters of the white sand beach are bordered by a cluster of palm trees that provide guests plenty of shade. The shallow, warm, and transparent waters of the Mediterranean Sea are ideal for swimming, sunbathing, and relaxation. While there is a wealth of marine life to be discovered, the beach is also excellent for snorkeling and scuba diving.

There is lots of parking at Vai Beach and it is accessible by vehicle or boat. Also available to visitors are buses from Sitia and boats from adjacent cities. Nearby cafés and taverns provide delicious Greek meals, fresh fish, and ice-cold beverages. For a modest price, visitors may also hire beach umbrellas and sun loungers.

One of the distinctive qualities of Vai Beach is that it is bordered by steep hills and cliffs, which give a wonderful background for photography and a spectacular perspective of the Mediterranean Sea. There are several routes that lead to isolated coves and hills that are perfect for trekking. Sitia and Palekastro, two neighboring towns, are also worthwhile visiting since they are full of history, culture, and delectable cuisine.

On the island of Crete, Vai Beach is a well-kept secret that is ideal for anybody looking for serenity and unspoiled beauty. Vai Beach is a spectacular experience with its clean seas, golden sand, and distinctive palm grove.

Preveli Beach

Preveli Beach, on the southern coast of Crete, is a lonely, undiscovered treasure. The beach is located near the Kourtaliotis River's mouth, and rocky mountains and sheer cliffs surround it. It is the ideal location for swimming and sunbathing due to the crystal-clear, emerald-green seas and smooth, white sand, while the neighboring palm grove offers shade and a beautiful background. From the adjacent settlement of Preveli, you may get to the beach by boat or by trekking.

On Crete's southern coast, Preveli Beach is a gorgeous, undeveloped beach. The beach is tucked away near the Kourtaliotis River's mouth, surrounded by jagged mountains and sheer cliffs. From the adjacent settlement of Preveli, you may get to the beach by boat or by trekking.

Preveli Beach's palm grove, which is located behind the beach and offers a lovely and tranquil location for guests to rest in the shade, is one of its most distinctive characteristics. Since they are indigenous to Crete, the palm palms give the island a unique tropical feel.

Preveli Beach's waters are the ideal color for swimming and snorkeling since they are clear and emerald green. Families with young children will find it to be the perfect location because of the warm, welcoming water and the beach's relative shallowness. Visitors may enjoy the calming sounds of the moderate waves while sunbathing and resting on the smooth, white beach.

Exploring the neighboring river and canyon is one of the joys of a trip to Preveli Beach. Tourists may take a leisurely trek around the canyon, which is encircled by high cliffs and a verdant landscape or go swimming in the cold, clear waters of the river.

There are several ways to go to Preveli Beach. Tourists may walk from the adjacent settlement of Preveli or take a boat from Plakias. A steep fall down a rocky trail is included in the walk, which lasts around an hour and a half. However, the drive is worthwhile because of the breathtaking surroundings.

A beach is a great place for people who want to get away from the throng and enjoy some peace and quiet since it is comparatively calm and isolated. Sun loungers and umbrellas, a seashore café, and a small bar are all accessible for those who need them, however.

Preveli Beach is an undiscovered treasure that shouldn't be missed. It is one of Crete's most stunning and tranquil beaches because of its distinctive palm grove, clean seas, and remote position. Preveli Beach is guaranteed to please you whether you're wanting to soak up the sun, explore the adjacent river and valley, or just take in the breathtaking environment.

Matala Beach

The southern shore of Crete's Matala Beach is a well-liked location for swimming, tanning, and people-watching. The coastline is well-known for its rocky caverns, which in the 1960s and 1970s served as dwellings for hippies and other free spirits. Nowadays, the beach is a perfect spot to unwind and take in the laid-back atmosphere and is home to various taverns, cafés, and gift stores.

Matala Beach, located on Crete's southern coast, is a stunning and distinctive beach with a long history. The rocky caverns on this beach, which served as houses for hippies and other free spirits in the 1960s and 1970s, are what make it so unique. For those who are interested in history and culture, these caverns are a fascinating sight and a must-visit location.

Aside from the caverns, Matala Beach has a lot to offer tourists. A vast stretch of fine sand beach is encircled by rocky cliffs and azure seas. It is the perfect location for swimming, people-watching, and sunbathing, and because of the shallow seas, it is a secure area for families with small children. The beachfront promenade, which is lined with cafés, pubs, and stores offering mementos and regional goods, is another place where visitors may wander.

The exploration of the caverns is one of the most well-liked activities in Matala Beach. When exploring the caverns, visitors may envision what life must have been like for the hippies who previously resided there. The caverns are a great place to see the sunset, and many tourists congregate there in the evenings to enjoy the breathtaking vistas.

Together with the caverns, Matala Beach is significant historically and culturally. Ancient Greek mythology made reference to the shore, and Odysseus, a well-known Greek hero, is claimed to have landed there. The beach served as a port during the Roman period, and several historical remains and relics have been discovered nearby.

There are various routes leading from Matala Beach into the neighboring hills and farmland for hikers to choose from. These paths are a wonderful way to explore the region and get some exercise at the same time since they provide breathtaking views of the beach and the surrounding area.

On the island of Crete, Matala Beach is a unique and lovely location that is well worth seeing. Each visitor to the island should go there because of its history, natural beauty, and cultural relevance. Everyone can find something to enjoy at Matala Beach, whether they're interested in exploring the caverns, lounging on the beach, or going on a trek through the nearby hills.

Agia Pelagia Beach

Families and couples like to go to Agia Pelagia Beach, which is on Crete's northern shore. The adjacent cliffs and rocky outcroppings offer a magnificent background, while the protected cove and tranquil seas make it a perfect place for swimming. There are several eateries, cafés, and gift stores along the shore.

A stunning and well-liked beach, Agia Pelagia Beach is situated on Crete's northern shore. It is well renowned for its protected harbor and tranquil waves, making it a fantastic vacation spot for couples and families looking to unwind at the beach. Beautiful hills and cliffs surround the shore, providing a stunning scene.

Agia Pelagia Beach's crystal-clear waters provide excellent swimming and snorkeling. Children may safely swim and play in the water at the bay since it is quiet and reasonably shallow. Other water sports including paddleboarding, kayaking, and windsurfing are also excellent on the beach. Rock climbing and cliff diving options are also provided by the bay's stunning granite formations and cliffs.

In addition to being a fantastic location to enjoy the ocean, Agia Pelagia Beach offers a ton of conveniences and recreational opportunities. Along the shore, there are a number of eateries and cafés that provide fresh seafood and traditional Greek fare, as well as pubs and nightclubs for those wishing to have a good time. A number of stores offering souvenirs, beachwear, and other goods are located near the beach.

There are several hiking trails and natural attractions close by for people who wish to explore more of the neighborhood. A few traditional taverns and little stores may be found in the nearby hamlet of Agia Pelagia, which is just a short walk away. In the stunning hills and mountains that surround the beach, visitors may also take a short trip to discover historic sites, secret caverns, and other natural treasures.

Agia Pelagia Beach is conveniently accessible by automobile or public transportation. The beach is situated about 20 kilometers west of Heraklion, the capital of Crete, and is just a 30-minute drive from the city center. Tourists may go from Heraklion to Agia Pelagia via cab or local bus as well. For those who decide to drive, there are a number of parking spaces close to the beach.

Visitors to Crete should visit Agia Pelagia Beach since it is stunning and easily accessible. It's a wonderful site to spend a day at the beach and explore the neighborhood because of the calm waves, breathtaking landscape, and range of activities available there.

Each beachgoer will be satisfied by the selection of stunning and distinctive beaches that Crete has to offer. The beaches of Crete offer something for everyone, whether you're seeking pink sand, palm palms, or rocky caverns.

The Minoan Palace of Knossos

On the Greek island of Crete is where you can find the Minoan Palace of Knossos. It is regarded as the biggest and most spectacular of the Minoan palaces and is one of the most significant and well-known archaeological sites in Greece. The palace was the hub of the Minoan civilization until it was destroyed in 1450 BC. It was constructed during the Bronze Age, circa 1900 BC.

A Cretan businessman called Minos Kalokairinos initially found the palace in 1878 while searching the region for antiquated antiquities. Yet serious excavations didn't start until 1900, under the direction of British archaeologist Arthur Evans. Evans spent a significant portion of his life studying and restoring the palace because he was captivated by the ancient Minoan civilization.

Around 20,000 square meters of structures and courtyards make up the enormous Minoan Palace of Knossos complex. The main entrance was situated on the second level of the palace's multi-level construction. Two substantial stone columns, together referred to as the "Pillar Crypt," which were once utilized for religious rites, flank the entrance.

There are a lot of rooms and hallways within the palace, including throne chambers, audience halls, storerooms, and dwelling quarters. Frescoes that portrayed scenes from daily life, religious rituals, and legendary events were painted on the palace's walls. The "Women in Blue," "Bull Leaping," and "Prince of the Lilies" are a few of the most well-known frescoes.

The central courtyard of the palace, which is ringed by columns and was originally utilized for public events and meetings, is one of its most outstanding features. The "Throne Chamber," where the monarch of Knossos would receive guests and hold court, is also located in the courtyard.

Stone, mudbrick, and wood were all combined in the construction of the palace. The wood used to build the elaborate roof structures and ornamental components were imported from neighboring Mediterranean countries, including Lebanon and Cyprus. The palace also included a sophisticated drainage and water management system, which was crucial given Crete's hot and dry environment.

The Minoan Palace of Knossos was finally destroyed, probably as a consequence of an earthquake or invasion, despite its magnificence and complexity. Prior to its rediscovery in the late 19th century, the palace had been abandoned and forgotten for thousands of years. Currently, the palace is a well-liked tourist destination that receives thousands of visitors each year.

The palace's maintenance and repair have been the subject of significant debate in recent years. Evans has come under fire from certain archaeologists and academics for his aggressive restoration methods, which they claim hid the palace's original characteristics. Others have backed Evans, saying that his restoration efforts were required to protect the palace for the next generations.

The Minoan Palace of Knossos is still a significant and intriguing archaeological monument, providing a window into the ancient civilization that once thrived on the island of Crete, notwithstanding the debates. The palace provides evidence of the Minoans' brilliance, creativity, and sophistication. The Minoans are known for their art, architecture, and culture, which still fascinates and inspires people today.

Chania: The Most Beautiful Town in Crete

On Crete's western shore sits the lovely town of Chania. It is one of the island's most visited tourist locations and is renowned for its

Venetian port, ancient town, lovely beaches, and breathtaking natural surroundings.

History of Chania:

Chania has a long history that dates back to the Minoan period. Over the years, Chania has been controlled by many different civilizations, notably the Venetians and the Ottomans. The town's ancient old town is a special and lovely site to visit since it still has numerous buildings and structures from the Venetian and Ottoman eras.

Venetian Port:

The Venetian harbor in Chania, which was built in the fourteenth century, is among the city's most well-known landmarks. Beautiful Venetian-era structures, like the lighthouse and the Firkas Fortress, which is now home to a marine museum, surround the harbor. The port is a well-liked tourist attraction due to the abundance of eateries, coffee shops, and bars there.

Historic Old Town:

The 14th-century Venetian harbor in Chania is among the city's most well-known landmarks. The lighthouse and the Firkas Fortress, which is now home to a marine museum, are just two of the stunning

Venetian-era structures that surround the harbor. The port is a well-liked tourist attraction since it also has a lot of dining establishments, coffee shops, and pubs.

Beautiful Beaches:

Moreover, Chania is renowned for having some of the nicest beaches on the island. Balos Lagoon, Elafonisi Beach, and Falassarna Beach are some of the most well-known beaches in Chania, and they are all nearby. The beaches are renowned for their glistening seas, powdery white sand, and breathtaking scenery.

Natural Surroundings:

The White Mountains and the Samaria Gorge are only two examples of the breathtaking natural splendor that surrounds Chania. With peaks up to 2,500 meters, the White Mountains are the island's tallest mountain range. Many historic towns, hiking paths, and ski areas may be found in the highlands. One of the most well-liked trekking spots on the island is the Samaria Gorge, a national park in the White Mountains.

Cuisine:

The ancient history and rich cultural legacy of the island have a big impact on Chania's exquisite food. Dakos, a typical Cretan salad, kalitsounia, a sort of cheese and herb pastry, and grilled octopus are a few of the must-try foods in Chania. Also, visitors may savor regional wines and alcoholic beverages like raki and tsikoudia.

Chania is a lovely town with fascinating past and breathtaking natural surroundings. Everyone can find something to do in Chania, whether they want to see the ancient town, relax on the beaches, or go trekking in the White Mountains. Chania is regarded as one of the most attractive cities in Crete, and it's not hard to understand why with its delectable food, bustling environment, and friendly people.

The Samaria Gorge: A Hiker's Paradise

On the Greek island of Crete's southwest coast sits the Samaria Gorge, a hiking paradise. One of the longest in Europe, the gorge is 18 kilometers long. It is renowned for its varied flora and wildlife and is also a UNESCO Biosphere Reserve. Every year, millions of tourists go to the Samaria Gorge to take in its spectacular beauty and enjoy the excitement of trekking across its challenging terrain.

In the White Mountains National Park, the Samaria Gorge is accessible from Omalos town. From here, hikers may take a bus to the gorge's entrance, which is 1,230 meters above sea level. The climb begins at the gorge's entrance, which is identified by a sign that says "Xyloskalo."

One hiking trek walk through the Samaria Gor, hiking hike through the Samaria Sam, Crete, C both both both both both both both both both both both hiking Crete C. C. Sam Sam Sam Sam Sam Sam Sam The route descends from a height of 1,230 meters to the seaside hamlet of Agia Roumeli, which is situated at sea level. Hikers will come across a variety of terrain along the trip, including rocky trails, wooden bridges, and constrained spaces. The trek needs a high degree of endurance and stamina since the terrain may be rough and steep.

A wide range of plants and animals, including rare and endangered species, may be found in the Samaria Gorge. Wild goats, badgers, and foxes are just a few of the creatures that visitors to the gorge could observe in addition to a variety of wildflowers, herbs, and trees. The critically endangered kri-kri, a kind of wild goat that can only be found on the island of Crete, calls the canyon home.

The "Iron Gates," a confined space that is barely four meters wide and 300 meters high, is the Samaria Gorge's most notable feature. The narrowest part of the gorge, this stunning corridor is a popular location for hikers to snap pictures. Midway along the trek, at the

"Iron Gates," is a fantastic spot to stop and take in the breathtaking landscape.

The trail ends at the seaside town of Agia Roumeli, which can only be reached on foot or by boat. The community attracts many hikers and provides a range of services, including dining establishments, coffee shops, and lodging. After a strenuous climb down the canyon, swimming and resting at the beach at Agia Roumeli are excellent options.

Samaria Gorge hiking needs thoughtful planning and preparation. Hikers should carry lots of water, a hat, and sunscreen, and they should wear sturdy shoes. Depending on the hiker's fitness level and speed, the trek might take anywhere from 4 to 7 hours to accomplish. While the route is well-marked and well-maintained, hikers should take care and stick to the prescribed path to prevent being hurt or lost.

In Crete, the Samaria Gorge is a must-see location for hikers and environment lovers. Visitors will have a remarkable and gratifying experience thanks to the breathtaking environment, varied flora and wildlife, and difficult terrain. The Samaria Gorge is a breathtaking natural marvel that should not be missed, regardless of your hiking experience.

Chapter 13: Crete's Regional Cuisines

Cretan Cuisine: Simple and Delicious

One of the most distinctive and delectable cuisines in the world, Cretan food is renowned for its simplicity, use of seasonal, locally produced products, and emphasis on healthy eating. The island of Crete's food is a significant part of its culture and history, reflecting both the island's lengthy history and the many conquerors and tourists it has received throughout the years.

The use of natural, fresh ingredients is one of the defining characteristics of Cretan cooking. Cretans enjoy access to a broad variety of locally produced fruits and vegetables, as well as fresh fish and high-quality meats, thanks to the island's rich soil, temperate temperature, and quantity of fresh water. Cretan food relies heavily on olive oil, which gives many meals a distinctive and delectable taste.

Dakos, a typical salad prepared with barley rusk, fresh tomatoes, and feta cheese, is one of the most well-known dishes in Cretan cuisine. The meal, which is topped with oregano and olive oil, is a superb illustration of the straightforward, natural tastes that are at the core of Cretan cooking.

Lamb with stamnagathi, a species of wild green found exclusively in Crete, is another traditional meal. Slow-cooking the delicate lamb with the bitter greens and a few basic ingredients produces a meal that is both tasty and nourishing.

Moreover, seafood plays a significant role in Cretan cooking, with fresh fish and shellfish dominating menus all around the island. Popular meals like grilled octopus, fried calamari, and sardines are often accompanied by a squeeze of lemon and a sprinkle of olive oil.

Another key ingredient in Cretan cooking is cheese, and the island offers a wide variety of delectable cheeses. Graviera, a hard cheese that is comparable to Gruyere or Parmesan, is one of the most well-liked varieties. The cheese, which is manufactured from sheep's milk, may be found in grilled cheese sandwiches as well as pastries and pies.

One of the most unusual elements of Cretan cuisine is the use of wild greens and herbs in numerous recipes. Oregano, thyme, and wild fennel are just a few of the many delicious plants and herbs that may be found on the island. These components are often used to enhance the taste and complexity of recipes, and they are also thought to provide a number of health advantages.

Cretan cuisine is renowned for its flavorful meals as well as its balanced and healthy eating philosophy. Several Cretan meals are abundant in vitamins, minerals, and other essential elements since the island has a long history of utilizing fresh, complete foods in their original condition. Many studies have examined the island's food, which has been linked to a number of health advantages, including a lower risk of heart disease and a few forms of cancer.

The natural splendor and lengthy history of the island are well reflected in Cretan cuisine. The island's long history of healthy eating and reverence for the land and sea are reflected in the food, which is straightforward, flavorful, and fresh. Cretan cuisine is certain to create a lasting impression, whether you're a food enthusiast or simply want to get a flavor of what Crete really tastes like.

Wine Tasting in Crete

Some of Europe's oldest vineyards may be found in Crete, which also has a long history of producing wine. The soil and temperature of the island provide the best conditions for a wide range of grape varieties, resulting in unique and tasty wines. Visitors may taste regional wines and discover the history of winemaking on the island of Crete via the popular pastime of wine tasting.

History of Wine in Crete:

For thousands of years, wine has played a significant role in Cretan culture and history. There is evidence of winemaking going back to the Minoan period, making the island one of the earliest places in Europe to plant grapes and create wine. The Minoans sold their wine all around the Mediterranean because of their highly developed culture and skill at sea.

Due to a lack of infrastructure, restricted technology, and a poor market for its wines, Crete has recently struggled to modernize its wine industry. Nonetheless, there has been a revival in interest in Cretan wines recently, and several vineyards and wineries have invested in marketing and modernization to support their distinctive goods.

Varieties of Cretan Wines:

Crete produces a wide range of wine varieties, including both red and white wines. Some of the most popular grape varieties used in Cretan wines include:

Vidiano: Vidiano is a white grape variety that is native to Crete. It produces wines that are floral and fruity, with notes of peach, pear, and apricot.

Vilana: Vilana is another white grape variety that is commonly used in Cretan wines. It produces wines that are light and fresh, with a citrusy flavor and aroma.

Kotsifali: Kotsifali is a red grape variety that is commonly grown in Crete. It produces wines that are medium-bodied with flavors of cherry, raspberry, and spices.

Mandilari: Mandilari is another red grape variety that is commonly used in Cretan wines. It produces wines that are full-bodied with notes of black fruit, spices, and chocolate.

Wine Tasting Tours in Crete:

Wine-tasting excursions are a well-liked method to discover the island's wine culture and try its distinctive wares. Tourists may take guided tours of vineyards and wineries where they can learn about the history of winemaking in Crete as well as the methods used to grow grapes and make wine. Many trips give provide the chance to sample and buy several wine varieties.

Some of the most popular wineries and vineyards in Crete include:

Lyrarakis Winery: The family-run Lyrarakis Winery has been making wines in the town of Alagni in the center of Crete since 1966. The winery is renowned for producing premium organic wines from conventional Cretan grape varietals.

Douloufakis Winery: The Douloufakis Winery is situated in the Heraklion area town of Dafnes. The winery is well-known for its acclaimed wines created from regional grape varietals including Kotsifali and Vidiano.

Manousakis Winery: The family-run Manousakis Winery, which makes both red and white wines, is situated in the hamlet of Vatolakos. The winery's distinctive mixes and usage of foreign grape varietals are well-known.

Domaine Paterianakis: In the town of Arkalochori, Domaine Paterianakis is well-known for its organic wines created from local grape varietals including Vidiano and Mandilari. Also, the winery provides tours and product samples.

Visitors to Crete may also discover the island's vineyards and wineries via wine excursions and tastings in addition to visiting wineries and vineyards. Winemaking has been practiced on the island of Crete for a very long time. The rocky topography and hot, dry climate of the island provide excellent grape-growing conditions, and Crete is home to numerous native grape types that are unique to the globe.

The region around the hamlet of Peza, which is situated just south of Heraklion, is one of the most well-known areas for wine sampling in Crete. Both red and white wines, especially the well-liked Vilana and Kotsifali kinds, are famous in this area. Guests may visit the vineyards, see how wine is made, and sample a range of wines.

Another popular region for wine tasting is the area around the town of Sitia, located on the eastern coast of Crete. This region is known for its dry red wines made from the Liatiko grape variety, as well as its white wines made from the Thrapsathiri and Vilana grape varieties. Visitors can take a tour of the local wineries and sample the wines, which are often paired with local cheese and other Cretan specialties.

Visitors to Crete may participate in wine festivals and activities all year long in addition to wine excursions and tastings. The Wine Festival of Dafnes, which takes place in August in the hamlet of Dafnes, which is close to Heraklion, is one of the most well-liked occasions. Live music, local wine tastings, and authentic Cretan cuisine are all part of the celebration.

Visitors may experience some of the greatest wines in the world while learning about the rich history and culture of the island of Crete via wine tasting. Crete is a must-visit location for wine enthusiasts and foodies alike because of its breathtaking environment, welcoming people, and mouthwatering wines.

Raki: Crete's Traditional Spirit

The ancient spirit of Crete, raki, sometimes referred to as tsikoudia, is a vital component of the island's gastronomic and cultural legacy. This clear, colorless liquid, whose history may be traced back to the island's ancient Minoan civilization, is made from the must of grapes or other fruits.

Raki manufacturing has a long history in Crete, where several families and localities produce their unique variations of alcoholic beverages. After grapes are harvested, they are crushed, and the juice that results is then usually left to ferment. Raki is made by distilling the fermented juice, or must, in a copper still.

Raki is often drunk as an aperitif or digestif, and it may also be used to enhance food while cooking. The alcohol percentage of the spirit, which may be between 40% and 65%, is high and it has a strong, unique flavor and scent.

Visits to local distilleries where raki is produced are among the greatest ways to enjoy the drink. Several small-scale distilleries welcome tourists and provide raki samples together with other regional goods like honey, olive oil, and herbs.

Moreover, raki is a mainstay during customary Cretan ceremonies including weddings, christenings, and festivals. It is often offered with meze, a spread of tiny dishes that may include cheese, cured meats, vegetables, olives, and cheese.

Raki has long been a significant part of the Cretan culture in addition to its culinary purposes. It is often used as a treatment for many illnesses in folk medicine, and it is said to have both therapeutic and aphrodisiac effects.

Many Cretans like sharing a bottle of raki with friends and family since it is a popular social drink in their culture. The custom of group drinking, or kouzina, is an essential element of Cretan culture and a significant means of bringing people together to honor their heritage.

For tourists to Crete, tasting raki is a must-try experience. Several eateries and tavernas on the island serve the spirit, and many neighborhood markets and stores offer bottles of handmade raki that tourists may buy as a memento.

Raki provides a window into Cretan history and customs in addition to its flavor and cultural value. Raki, one of the oldest and most popular alcoholic drinks on the island, is a significant element of the community's history and a representation of the Cretan way of life.

Cooking Classes in Crete

In addition to its breathtaking scenery, ancient monuments, and gorgeous beaches, Crete is also known for its delectable and healthful food. Taking a cooking class in Crete is a great way to become acquainted with the island's culinary tradition whether you're a gourmet or simply curious about the regional cuisine. Here we will discuss the many culinary school options in Crete and what to anticipate from each.

Traditional Cretan Cooking Classes:

Classes in traditional Cretan cookery provide a real-world and realistic culinary experience. You'll discover how to make traditional meals like Dakos, Moussaka, and Pastitsio using fresh regional ingredients. Also, you'll discover traditional cooking methods as well as the meals' historical and cultural value. As most sessions are conducted in local houses, you may get a taste of Cretan hospitality and way of life.

Olive Oil Tasting and Cooking Classes:

One of the healthiest oils in the world, olive oil is a main component of Cretan cuisine. A wonderful approach to learning about the many kinds of olive oils, their tastes, and how to utilize them in cooking is to take cooking and olive oil tasting lessons. Also, you'll discover how to prepare classic meals like grilled vegetables with olive oil, tomato, and olive salad, and feta cheese and olive oil dip.

Wine Tasting and Cooking Classes:

Some top-notch wineries that create fine wines are located in Crete. Learning about the island's wine culture and history while preparing a tasty dinner is made possible via wine tasting and culinary workshops. You'll discover the many kinds of wines made on the island, how to match them with meals, and how to prepare meals with wine. Also, you'll get practical experience cooking traditional Cretan cuisine from scratch using regional and seasonal ingredients.

Vegetarian and Vegan Cooking Classes:

Cretan food is renowned for emphasizing natural, fresh ingredients, making it a fantastic option for vegetarians and vegans. Cooking lessons in Crete for vegetarians and vegans provide an opportunity to learn how to create delectable plant-based meals using regional and seasonal ingredients. You'll learn about various herbs and spices, how to utilize them in recipes, and how to put together wholesome nutritious meals.

Seafood Cooking Classes:

Being an island, Crete relies heavily on fish in its cuisine. Learning to make tasty meals with fresh fish from the area's harvest is possible via seafood cooking workshops. You'll discover the many varieties of fish, along with its cleaning, preparing, and traditional Cretan cooking techniques. Also, you'll discover how to mix seafood meals with regional wines as well as other seafood flavors.

A great approach to discovering Crete's culinary heritage and culture is to enroll in a cooking class. There is a cooking lesson for everyone, whether you're interested in learning how to prepare traditional Cretan food, olive oil tasting, wine tasting, vegetarian and vegan cookery, or seafood preparation. You'll gain new knowledge, make new friends, and savor delectable meals and beverages. So why not arrange a cooking lesson in Crete to liven up your vacation?

Chapter 14: Insider Tips for Traveling in Greece

The Best Time to Visit Greece

Greece is a stunning nation that welcomes millions of tourists each year. Greece is a tourist destination that attracts visitors of all ages and interests due to its breathtaking scenery, extensive history, lively culture, and delectable food. Perhaps one of the most crucial factors to think about while organizing a vacation to Greece is scheduling. This is a guide that considers the weather, people, and special events to determine when is the ideal time to go to Greece.

High Season (June-August)

Greece's busiest travel months are June through August. Swimming, sunbathing, and other outdoor activities are ideal in this season due to the warm, sunny weather. Booking lodging and activities well in advance is essential due to the crowded beaches and bustling nature of famous tourist locations. While planning your trip's budget, bear in mind that prices for flights, lodging, and activities are also higher during this time.

Shoulder Season (May and September)

Greece's May through mid-June and September through mid-October shoulder seasons are ideal times to go there. Even if it's still nice and bright outside, there are fewer people around and costs are often cheaper than they are in the high season. Without the crowds, now is a fantastic time to see the nation's historical monuments, climb through the highlands, or visit the islands. It's important to keep in mind that some of the smaller islands could have fewer ferry connections at this time, so it's a good idea to double-check ahead of time.

Low Season (November-April)

Greece's low season, which lasts from November to April, may not be ideal for swimming and tanning, but it's fantastic for seeing the nation's towns, monuments, and museums. At this period, the weather may be erratic, with some days being chilly and wet while others are still sunny. At this time, there are fewer people around and lodging, travel, and activity costs are at their lowest.

Seasonal Events

Greece is a nation that enjoys partying, so you might consider scheduling your vacation around a few seasonal celebrations. These are some of the most well-liked:

Carnival: Parades, parties, and masquerade balls are held all around Greece during this major celebration. Patras, which is renowned for its vibrant parades and exciting parties, hosts the world's most well-known Carnival events.

Easter: Easter is the most important Christian festival in Greece, and it is widely observed throughout. Processions, religious services, and feasts take place the week before Easter Sunday. It's customary to roast a lamb on a spit and gather with loved ones for a substantial meal on Easter Sunday.

Summer Festivals: Over the summer, many Greek villages and cities offer cultural events that include theater, dance, and music. One of the most well-known festivals is the Athens and Epidaurus

Festival, which offers a schedule of plays, concerts, and dance performances in historic theaters.

Your hobbies, spending power, and travel preferences will determine the ideal time to visit Greece. Peak season is the ideal time to go if you want to enjoy beaches, swimming, and sunlight. The shoulder season or low season, on the other hand, is the best time to go if you'd rather stay away from the crowds and save money. Greece is a beautiful nation with a lot to offer, including ancient history, stunning natural scenery, delectable cuisine, and friendly locals, no matter what time of year you decide to visit.

Money-Saving Tips for Traveling in Greece

Greece is a wonderful and fascinating nation with a lot to offer visitors, including gorgeous beaches, picture-perfect cities, ancient ruins, and delectable food. While visiting Greece might be a little pricey, there are plenty of methods to save costs without compromising the value of your vacation. Here are some suggestions for visiting Greece while saving money:

The off-season is the best time to visit since rates for lodgings, airfare, and activities are often substantially higher during Greece's busiest travel months of June through August. If you want to travel on a budget, think about going in the off-season (November to

March) or shoulder season (April to May and September to October), when costs are cheaper and crowds are lighter.

Use public transportation: In Greece, particularly during the busy season, taxis and vehicle rentals may be pricey. Instead, think about using cheaper and more dependable public transit like buses or the metro. A fun and environmentally responsible method to move about is to hire a bike, which is offered by many towns and cities.

A variety of lodging options are available in Greece, from high-end resorts to affordable hostels and guesthouses. Budget lodging options, such as hostels, guesthouses, or flats, are often less expensive than hotels if you're trying to save money. Also, you may save money by making reservations in advance or by staying away from the busiest tourist spots.

Dine like a local: Greek food is delectable and diversified, and many of the classic meals are great and reasonably priced. Find neighborhood eateries and taverns that sell classic foods like souvlaki, moussaka, or Greek salad to save costs on meals. Eating fast food or buying for groceries to make your own meals at nearby markets and supermarkets are further ways to save costs.

Take advantage of free activities: Greece is home to several free attractions and activities, like seeing historic sites and ancient ruins, climbing in the mountains, and swimming at the beach. The Acropolis in Athens, trekking the Samaria Gorge in Crete and seeing

Chania's ancient town are a few of the best free things to do in Greece.

Keep an eye on your spending: It's simple to get carried away with the adventure of traveling and splurge on attractions, meals, and souvenirs. Make a budget before your trip and do your best to adhere to it to prevent overpaying. To keep tabs on your expenditures and get discounts on attractions and lodging, you may use utilize apps or websites.

Search for special offers and discounts. Several Greek attractions and activities provide discounts for individuals, families, and groups, as well as bundles and other bargains. Check for package offers that include lodging, activities, and transportation, or look for discounts on activities like museum visits, boat excursions, or water sports.

Dealing with vendors is customary in Greece, particularly when purchasing souvenirs and other things from sellers at marketplaces and bazaars. Be kind and considerate, and be prepared to leave if you can't come to an agreement on a price. By purchasing food and other necessities in your neighborhood markets and supermarkets, you may also save money.

With little preparation and careful budgeting, traveling in Greece can be both inexpensive and fun. You may save costs and enjoy your vacation to Greece by using public transit, finding inexpensive lodging and Greek food, as well as by seeking deals and cost-free activities.

How to Avoid Crowds at Popular Attractions

Although visiting well-known tourist locations might be exhilarating, navigating crowds can be a real pain. Your entire experience may be hampered by long lines, congested areas, and restricted access to popular activities. Here are some suggestions for avoiding crowds and enjoying your visit if you're planning a vacation to a well-known location.

Visiting During Off-Season

To escape crowds, one of the greatest strategies is to go off-peak. Typically, this is the period of the year when the weather is less than ideal and there are fewer visitors. The busiest months in Greece are from mid-June to mid-September, so if you can, try to go in May or October to avoid the crowds.

Go Early or Late

Visiting major locations early in the morning or late in the day may also help you escape crowds. By coming early or remaining later, you may avoid the crowds since many visitors often sleep in or have lunch at these hours. Also, the light at certain times of day may be lovely and provide fantastic picture opportunities.

Book in Advance

You may also avoid crowds by making reservations in advance for your excursions or tickets. Booking in advance assures that you'll have a place booked and won't have to wait in line since many sites and trips have limited capacity. Also, you may often avoid the ticket office by making your reservations online, which can save you time.

Take a Guided Tour

You can escape the crowds while still learning interesting facts and details about the destination you're visiting by joining a guided tour. Tour guides often have privileged access to off-limits locations or may give you a more personalized experience. They may also assist you in navigating the throng more effectively.

Explore Less Popular Attractions

If you want to completely escape crowds, think about visiting less well-known locations. Even if they may not be as well-known or well-known as the well-known landmarks, they can nonetheless provide intriguing and distinctive experiences. You'll also have an opportunity to meet people from the area and get a more genuine taste of its culture.

Use the Public Transit

Using public transit might be an economical option to avoid crowds while visiting a city. The city center is home to several well-liked tourist attractions, although parking and traffic there may be a challenge. You may save time and stress by using public transit, and you'll be able to explore the city like a resident.

Enjoy a Break

Lastly, take a break if you find yourself in a busy environment and are feeling overstimulated. Take a seat in a calm area, get food or beverage, and unwind for a while. When you're prepared, you'll feel more calm and prepared to face the masses.

There are various methods to get to well-known locations without encountering crowds. You may make the most of your vacation while avoiding the stress of crowds by visiting during the off-season, traveling early or late, reserving in advance, taking a guided tour, discovering less well-known locations, utilizing public transit, and taking pauses. Never forget to be adaptable and open-minded, and try not to let the masses spoil your trip.

Tips for Traveling with Children in Greece

Greece is an excellent vacation spot for families with young children. There is something for everyone to enjoy in this region with its stunning beaches, historic sites, and vibrant culture. Planning beforehand can help to make your vacation as easygoing and stress-free as possible, but traveling with kids may still be difficult.

Here is some advice for families visiting Greece.

Choose a family-friendly hotel. It's crucial to choose family-friendly lodgings while traveling with kids. Try to choose lodgings that have features like swimming pools, kid-friendly activities, and childcare services. If you want more space and solitude than a hotel room can provide, think about renting a vacation house or apartment.

Bring water and snacks. It's crucial to be hydrated and well-fed when traveling, particularly with youngsters. While going on day outings, be sure to stock up on supplies and bring a lot of food and drinks with you.

Organize your schedule well. Pace your activities and avoid attempting to accomplish too much in one day while traveling with kids. Be sure to give yourself enough time for breaks and leisure while planning your schedule. Think about going to kid-friendly destinations like zoos, water parks, or theme parks.

Travel light. It's simple to overpack while traveling with kids. Yet, it might be challenging to handle a sleepy youngster while carrying big luggage and baggage. Try to simply bring the necessities and pack them lightly.

Think about using a guide. While seeing historical sites and museums, a skilled guide may make a world of difference. These can hold your kids' attention and improve everyone's enjoyment and learning from the event.

Be adaptable. Children are unpredictable, so things don't always go as planned. Being adaptable and going with the flow is crucial, even if it means straying from your plan.

Provide amusement. Kids may quickly get bored, particularly on lengthy car trips or airplanes. Bring them games, novels, and other entertainment to keep them busy and content.

Take security measures. Despite the fact that Greece is a secure nation, it is still advisable to exercise care while traveling with kids. Always keep a watch on your kids, particularly in busy places. Ensure that they are aware of what to do if they get lost or separated from you.

Observe regional customs. It's crucial to respect regional traditions and customs since Greece has a rich cultural past. Inspire your kids to respect and courtesy of locals by teaching them about Greek history and culture.

Have a wonderful time! Even though it might be difficult, traveling with kids can be a lot of fun. Spend quality time with your family and make lifelong memories.

Part VI: Accommodation and Eating Out

Chapter 15: Accommodation Options in Greece

Hotels

Greece is a well-liked vacation spot with a variety of lodging choices to fit any budget or desire. There are several possibilities, ranging from high-end resorts to inexpensive accommodations.

Hotels are a common lodging option in Greece, especially in metropolitan areas and well-known tourist locations. They provide a variety of facilities and services to meet the requirements and preferences of visitors. Greece has a strong heritage of hospitality and tourists to the nation can anticipate warm and welcoming treatment in most hotels.

One of the perks of staying at a hotel is the choice of room kinds offered. The hotel offers single, double, and twin rooms in addition to suites, which often include a separate living room and kitchenette. Depending on the cost and location of the hotel, the size and design of the rooms might vary substantially.

The majority of hotels in Greece are kept up well, are spotless, and provide daily cleaning services. The majority of hotels also include complimentary Wi-Fi, television, and air conditioning. A swimming pool, spa services, and a fitness center might be considered additional amenities. Moreover, some hotels feature on-site eateries, coffee shops, and bars that provide guests with a convenient and welcoming eating environment.

The location, time of year, and degree of luxury all affect the cost of hotels in Greece. All around the nation, especially in smaller towns and cities, are hotels that are affordable. These accommodations provide the bare necessities but may not include extras like a restaurant or pool. Mid-range lodgings often include additional features and are close to well-known tourist attractions. Larger cities and famous tourist locations, like the Greek islands, are home to luxury hotels and resorts.

It's crucial to think about a hotel's location and accessibility to surrounding attractions when reserving a hotel in Greece. Greek hotels are widely distributed around the country, making it simple for visitors to explore the region. Several hotels also provide tours and excursions that let visitors experience the local way of life.

By making hotel reservations in advance, guests may often save money. Early bird specials and package offers, which could include complimentary breakfast or other perks, are readily available at many hotels in Greece. To receive benefits and savings on subsequent visits, travelers may also think about signing up for hotel loyalty programs or utilizing hotel booking services.

Customer service quality is a different aspect to take into account when booking a hotel in Greece. Several hotels in Greece are run and managed by families, providing individualized service and a warm environment. Greek hotels often provide bilingual staff members who may suggest nearby sights to see, places to eat at, and activities to attend.

Knowing the local laws and traditions is crucial while staying at a hotel in Greece. At certain hotels, visitors are requested to take off their shoes before going inside their rooms, and smoking may not be permitted in particular locations. A pleasant and polite environment for all visitors is ensured by quiet hours and other regulations at many hotels.

All sorts of guests may find the facilities and services they require at hotels in Greece. Travelers may choose the ideal hotel that suits their needs and budget with a little preparation and study, and they can have a relaxing and pleasurable vacation in Greece.

Ten hotels in Greece are listed below that provide visitors with an excellent mix of quality and value:

Astra Suites, Santorini: a magnificent hotel with breathtaking views of the surrounding Caldera and the Aegean Sea. The hotel has a swimming pool, a fine-dining restaurant, and roomy rooms with private balconies. Costs per night start at around €450.

Ikos Dassia, Corfu: a family-friendly resort with all-inclusive deals and a variety of attractions, such as several pools, a private beach, a spa, and many dining options. Costs per night start at around €300.

Cavo Tagoo, Mykonos: A boutique hotel with cutting-edge style and opulent features including a magnificent infinity pool, a spa, and a rooftop bar with expansive island views. Rates for a night start at around €350.

Elounda Beach Hotel, Crete: a luxurious resort with private beaches, a spa, several pools, and a number of restaurants serving great cuisine. In addition, the hotel offers a variety of activities, such as tennis, golf, and water sports. Costs for a night start at around €500.

Grace Hotel, Santorini: A magnificent hotel with wonderful views of the surrounding island of Thirassia and the Caldera. The hotel has opulent rooms, a pool, a spa, and a fine dining restaurant. Costs for a night start at around €500.

Domes of Elounda, Crete: A family-friendly resort with a spa, many swimming pools, private beaches, and fine-dining restaurants. In addition, the hotel offers a variety of activities, such as tennis, golf, and water sports. Costs for a night start at around €400.

Costa Navarino, Messinia: An opulent resort with a spa, many swimming pools, private beaches, and fine dining restaurants. In addition, the hotel offers a variety of activities, such as tennis, golf, and water sports. Costs for a night start at around €400.

Santorini Secret Suites and Spa: A luxurious hotel with breathtaking views of the surrounding island of Thirassia and the Caldera. Elegant rooms with separate outdoor hot tubs, a pool, and a spa are available at the hotel. Costs for a night start at around €400.

Canaves Oia Epitome, Santorini: A boutique hotel with cutting-edge style and opulent features including a magnificent infinity pool, a spa, and a rooftop bar with expansive island views. Costs for a night start at around €500.

Casa Cook, Rhodes: A chic hotel with a laid-back, bohemian vibe with a variety of facilities, such as a restaurant, a spa, and a pool.

The hotel provides easy access to the adjacent town of Lindos and is situated close to a number of beaches. Costs per night start at around $250.

For tourists searching for quality and value in their accommodations, these hotels provide a variety of facilities and services to make your trip to Greece pleasant and memorable.

Resorts

For those looking for an opulent and pleasant holiday, resorts in Greece are a great option. They provide a variety of facilities and services, making them the ideal location to unwind, rest, and enjoy some pampering.

Blue Palace, a Luxury Collection Resort & Spa, Crete

Blue Palace, an opulent resort with breathtaking views of the Aegean Sea and the island of Spinalonga, is situated on the lovely island of Crete. There are 251 rooms and suites at the hotel, each having a balcony or terrace to themselves. Several swimming pools, a private beach, a spa, a fitness facility, and a variety of eating choices are available as amenities.

Daios Cove Luxury Resort & Villas, Crete

On the island of Crete, there is an opulent resort called Daios Cove. Each of the 300 guestrooms, suites, and villas at the resort has its own balcony or terrace with views of the ocean. The resort has a number of pools, a private beach, a spa, a fitness center, and a selection of restaurants.

Costa Navarino, Messinia

A luxurious resort called Costa Navarino may be found in Messinia, a stunning area in the Peloponnese. A variety of lodging choices are available at the resort, including rooms, suites, and villas, all of which have breathtaking views of the Ionian Sea or the resort's gardens. Several swimming pools, a private beach, a spa, golf courses, and a variety of food establishments are available as amenities.

Elounda Beach Hotel & Villas, Crete

On the island of Crete, there is an opulent resort called Elounda Beach Hotel & Villas. A range of lodging choices is available at the resort, including rooms, suites, and villas, each of which has its own balcony or patio. Several swimming pools, a private beach, a spa, a fitness facility, and a variety of eating choices are available as amenities.

Nikki Beach Resort & Spa, Porto Heli

In the Peloponnese village of Porto Heli, there lies a magnificent resort called Nikki Beach Resort & Spa. There are 66 rooms and suites available at the resort, each with its own balcony or patio. Several swimming pools, a private beach, a spa, a fitness facility, and a variety of eating choices are available as amenities.

Santa Marina, a Luxury Collection Resort, Mykonos

On the island of Mykonos, there is a beautiful resort called Santa Marina. Each of the resort's 101 guestrooms, suites, and villas has its own balcony or patio with breathtaking Aegean Sea views. Several swimming pools, a private beach, a spa, a fitness facility, and a variety of eating choices are available as amenities.

Myconian Utopia Resort, Mykonos

On the island of Mykonos, there is an opulent resort called Myconian Paradise Resort. There are 35 guestrooms and suites available at the resort, each with its own balcony or patio with awe-inspiring views of the Aegean Sea. Several swimming pools, a private beach, a spa, a fitness facility, and a variety of eating choices are available as amenities.

Grand Resort Lagonissi, Athens

On the Athenian Riviera, there is an opulent resort called Grand Resort Lagonissi. A range of lodging choices is available at the resort, including rooms, suites, and villas, all of which have breathtaking views of the Saronic Gulf. Several swimming pools, a private beach, a spa, a fitness facility, and a variety of eating choices are available as amenities.

Amanzoe, Porto Heli

In the Peloponnese village of Porto Heli, there is an opulent resort called Amanzoe. There are 38 pavilions available at the resort, each with a private pool and breathtaking views of the Aegean Sea. Amenities include of

Villas and Apartments

For those searching for more room, privacy, and freedom during their time in Greece, villas and apartments are a great choice. With its own private facilities, visitors may have a relaxing and individualized experience that can meet their unique demands.

Several of the villas and apartments in Greece are situated in picturesque places and provide breathtaking views of the sea or the mountains. There are many different facilities available in these residences, which may vary from modest flats to grand villas.

The freedom that renting a villa or apartment provides is one of its advantages. There are no regular mealtimes or timetables to adhere to, and guests are free to come and go as they want. Families with children or groups of friends who may have various schedules or tastes will find this to be very useful.

The extra space that villas and flats provide is another benefit. Villas and apartments provide plenty of space to stretch out, rest, and decompress in contrast to hotel rooms, which may sometimes seem claustrophobic. Villas are perfect for families and groups since they often feature many bedrooms and bathrooms, as well as living rooms, dining rooms, and outside spaces.

Greece offers a diversity of villa and apartment types and pricing points, making them affordable for tourists of all means. Although some houses could have more basic features, others might have more upscale features like outdoor kitchens, hot tubs, and private pools.

Greece's island of Santorini, which is renowned for its lovely whitewashed structures and breathtaking sunsets, is a popular location for homes and apartments. With many of the island's homes and apartments set into the cliffs, Santorini offers visitors breathtaking views of the caldera and the Aegean Sea.

The island of Crete is another well-liked location for homes and flats. Crete provides a range of residences to select from, including historic stone houses and contemporary, minimalist villas, thanks to its beautiful shoreline and picturesque landscape. Several of the villas in Crete have their own gardens and swimming pools, and some even have their own vineyards and olive trees.

In addition to Santorini and Crete, several villas and apartments are also offered in other well-known Greek locations including Mykonos, Corfu, and Rhodes. These homes vary in size and design from little flats located in the middle of the city to grand villas situated in the countryside.

It's crucial to take your unique requirements and tastes into account while selecting a villa or apartment in Greece. Although some houses could be more suited for couples or gatherings of friends, others might be more appropriate for families with small children. It's crucial to do some research on the property's location and how close it is to nearby landmarks, eateries, and beaches.

Both local property management firms and internet booking sites like Airbnb, HomeAway, and VRBO provide a variety of villas and flats for rent in Greece. When making a reservation, it's crucial to read reviews and do research to be sure the property will match your needs and be run by a reliable business.

For visitors to Greece, villas and apartments are a common and practical choice. These homes provide a customized and pleasant experience that can accommodate each visitor's unique requirements and preferences because of their increased space, privacy, and facilities. There are many homes to select from, in all types and pricing ranges, to ensure that you enjoy the ideal Greek vacation whether you're traveling with family, friends, or as a couple.

Here are 10 suggestions for good villas and apartments in Greece:

Villa Kyma, Mykonos - Agios Ioannis, Mykonos, 84600, Greece

This luxurious villa features five bedrooms, a private pool, and stunning views of the Aegean Sea.

The Architect's Villa, Santorini - Megalochori, Santorini, 84700, Greece

This unique villa was designed by a renowned Greek architect and features two bedrooms, a private pool, and a rooftop terrace with incredible views of the caldera.

Villa Mare e Monti, Corfu - Agios Gordios, Corfu, 49084, Greece

This villa offers panoramic views of the sea and the mountains and features four bedrooms, a private pool, and a large outdoor space for dining and relaxing.

The Hidden House, Crete - Episkopi, Rethymnon, 74100, Greece

This beautifully renovated traditional Cretan house features three bedrooms, a private pool, and a large outdoor space with stunning views of the countryside.

Villa Erato, Zakynthos - Pantokratoras, Zakynthos, 29091, Greece

This modern villa features five bedrooms, a private pool, and a large outdoor space with a barbecue and dining area.

Windmill Villas, Rhodes - Haraki, Rhodes, 85102, Greece

These unique villas are housed in traditional windmills and feature private pools and stunning sea views.

Sunset Suites, Paros - Naousa, Paros, 84401, Greece

These stylish and modern suites are just a short walk from the beach and offer views of the sea and the nearby town of Naousa.

Villa Alexandra, Crete - Vamos, Chania, 73008, Greece

This charming villa features three bedrooms, a private pool, and a large outdoor space with a barbecue and dining area.

The Cliff House, Zakynthos - Skinari, Zakynthos, 29091, Greece

This stunning villa is perched on a cliff overlooking the sea and features four bedrooms, a private pool, and a large outdoor space for dining and relaxing.

Apartments La Mer, Naxos - Agios Prokopios, Naxos, 84300, Greece

These modern apartments are just a short walk from the beach and offer comfortable accommodations with views of the sea and the nearby town of Agios Prokopios.

Camping

Greece's breathtaking natural beauty may be seen firsthand by camping there, which is a terrific option for those on a tight budget. Greece is home to a large number of campsites that let tourists set up camp in picturesque settings close to mountains, beaches, and other natural attractions. Here are some tips for camping in Greece as well as some of the top places to stay while planning your next vacation.

Facilities and Amenities:

The majority of campsites in Greece include basic amenities including bathrooms, showers, and power. Depending on their location and size, some campsites can feature restaurants, swimming pools, and other facilities. It's a good idea to do some research on campsites ahead of time to learn about the amenities they provide and the neighboring activities.

Camping Gear:

Don't worry if you don't have your own camping equipment. You don't need to carry your own as many campsites in Greece rent out tents, sleeping bags, and other supplies. Instead, you may rent equipment from businesses that specialize in outdoor activities or buy camping supplies from outdoor shops in Greece.

Campground Etiquette:

When camping in Greece, it's important to follow some basic rules to respect the natural environment and other campers. These rules include:

- Only set up your tent in designated areas.
- Do not light fires outside of designated fire pits or designated areas.
- Do not leave trash or litter in the campground or surrounding area.
- Respect quiet hours and keep noise levels down, especially at night.
- Be aware of local wildlife and respect their habitats.
- Do not harm or destroy any plants or trees.
- Best Campgrounds in Greece:

Camping Gythion Bay - Located in the Peloponnese region, this campground is situated on a beautiful beach and offers a range of activities, including beach volleyball, paddle boarding, and windsurfing.

Camping Sithonia - Located on the Sithonia peninsula in Halkidiki, this campground is surrounded by olive groves and offers access to a private beach. It's a great spot for families, with a playground, basketball court, and other activities for kids.

Camping Stavros - Located in northern Greece, this campground is situated in a forested area near the sea. It offers a range of outdoor activities, including hiking, fishing, and boating.

Camping Navarino - Located in the Peloponnese region, this campground is situated on a sandy beach and offers access to the nearby Voidokilia Bay. It's a great spot for those who want to enjoy water sports, like windsurfing and kiteboarding.

Camping Vrachos - Located on the Ionian coast, this campground offers stunning views of the sea and is situated near a beautiful beach. It's a great spot for those who want to enjoy swimming and sunbathing.

Camping Kalamitsi - Located on the southern tip of the Sithonia peninsula in Halkidiki, this campground is situated in a pine forest and offers access to a private beach. It's a great spot for those who want to enjoy the outdoors and explore the nearby mountains.

Camping Lichnos - Located on the Ionian coast, this campground is situated near a sandy beach and offers a range of water sports and other activities. It's a great spot for families, with a playground, volleyball court, and other amenities.

Camping Natura - Located on the island of Corfu, this campground is situated on a sandy beach and offers access to a range of outdoor activities, including hiking, fishing, and kayaking.

Camping Laconia - Located in the Peloponnese region, this campground is situated near the sea and offers access to a private beach. It's a great spot for those who love to be surrounded by nature and prefer a more budget-friendly option for accommodation. Camping in Greece allows visitors to experience the country's natural beauty and explore the great outdoors, while also enjoying a sense of community with other campers.

The variety of settings accessible is one of the key advantages of camping in Greece. There are campsites for every taste, including those along the ocean and others up in the mountains. A lot of campgrounds are found in national parks, giving guests access to some of the nation's most breathtaking natural landscapes, including woods, lakes, and rivers.

The majority of Greek campsites have access to power, water, and basic amenities like restrooms and showers. However, some campsites include more comprehensive facilities including restaurants, playgrounds, and swimming pools. When making a reservation, it's critical to confirm that the amenities will fit your requirements.

Travelers may also save money by going camping. In Greece, camping is much less expensive than staying at a hotel or resort, and many campgrounds provide discounts for extended stays. Also, camping enables visitors to cook their own food, which may reduce the cost of eating out.

The island of Crete is one of the most well-liked locations for camping in Greece. There are a number of campsites on the island that provide a variety of facilities and services. The following are a few of the top campsites in Crete:

- Camping Elizabeth is located in the village of Mirthios in the southern part of the island. The campground has stunning views of the Libyan Sea and offers facilities such as a swimming pool and a restaurant.
- Camping Chania, located on the west coast of Crete in the town of Chania. The campground is within walking distance of the beach and offers facilities such as a swimming pool, a bar, and a restaurant.
- Camping Paleochora, located in the town of Paleochora in the southern part of the island. The campground is situated on a hill with views of the sea and offers facilities such as a swimming pool and a restaurant.

- Camping Rethymno, located on the north coast of the island in the town of Rethymno. The campground is within walking distance of the beach and offers facilities such as a swimming pool, a restaurant, and a mini-market.

- Camping Sissi is located on the north coast of the island in the town of Sissi. The campground is situated on a hill with views of the sea and offers facilities such as a swimming pool and a restaurant.

- Camping Iraklia, located on the small island of Iraklia in the Cyclades. The campground is situated on a beautiful sandy beach and offers basic facilities, including showers and toilets.

- Camping Kouremenos is located on the east coast of the island in the town of Sitia. The campground is within walking distance of the beach and offers facilities such as a restaurant and a mini-market.

- Camping Finikes is located on the west coast of the island in the town of Kastelli Kissamos. The campground is situated on a hill with views of the sea and offers facilities such as a swimming pool and a restaurant.

- Camping Thines is located on the east coast of the island in the town of Vassiliki. The campground is situated on a hill with views of the sea and offers facilities such as a swimming pool and a restaurant.

- Camping Sikia is located on the west coast of the island in the town of Agios Nikolaos. The campground is situated on a hill with views of the sea and offers facilities such as a swimming pool, a bar, and a restaurant.

- Camping in Greece is a great option for travelers who want to experience the natural beauty of the country while

Hostels

In Greece, hostels have grown to be a preferred lodging choice for tourists on a tight budget. Hostels are an excellent option for backpackers, lone travelers, and groups of friends seeking a cheap place to stay because of their reasonable pricing, communal atmospheres, and handy locations.

The majority of the country's largest cities, including Athens, Thessaloniki, and Heraklion, as well as a large number of smaller towns and tourist hotspots, have hostels. They serve as an ideal launching point for exploring the neighborhood since they are often found in busy downtown locations near major transit hubs and tourist attractions.

Hostels provide a range of lodging options, including private rooms and dorms with either communal or private bathrooms. With prices beginning at around 10-15 euros per night, dorms are the most economical choice; individual rooms are more costly but still much less expensive than hotel rooms. Some hostels also have private, pleasant rooms with bathrooms, which are nonetheless less expensive than regular hotels.

The social environment in a hostel is one of its major benefits. The majority of hostels feature communal facilities where visitors may relax and meet other travelers from across the globe, including lounges, kitchens, and outdoor areas. Hostels often plan social gatherings that provide guests a chance to mingle and meet new people, such as pub crawls, city excursions, and game evenings. As a result, hostels are a fantastic option for lone travelers seeking travel companions.

The variety of facilities that hostels provide is another benefit. Although the majority of hostels provide the bare necessities like free Wi-Fi, lockers, and baggage storage, many also provide extras like laundry rooms, book exchanges, and even swimming pools or hot tubs. Some hostels provide complimentary breakfast as well, while others include on-site cafés and bars where guests may purchase food and beverages at reasonable costs.

Hostels are a fantastic choice for visitors on a budget, but there are a few disadvantages. Lack of privacy is one of the main problems. Dorm rooms may be loud and congested, and if your roommates are coming and going all through the night, it can be tough to get a decent night's sleep. Private rooms provide additional solitude, but since they are still part of a shared space, noise may still be a concern.

The absence of security in hostels is another possible drawback. Although the majority of hostels have security cameras and lockers, theft may still be a concern, particularly in dorm rooms where travelers share a space with strangers. It's crucial to take security measures, including locking up your possessions with a padlock and never leaving valuables alone.

For budget-conscious tourists seeking a friendly environment and a convenient location, hostels are a terrific option. They are a pleasant and unique way to discover Greece since they provide a variety of facilities and the chance to interact with tourists from all over the globe.

Here are 10 hostels in Greece that offer affordable and comfortable accommodations:

- **Athens Backpackers -** 12 Makri St, Athens: This centrally located hostel in Athens offers private rooms and dorms, as well as a rooftop terrace and bar.

- **Santorini Hostel -** Fira, Santorini: This hostel is located in the heart of Fira and offers private rooms and dorms, a swimming pool, and a sun terrace with views of the Aegean Sea.

- **Lub d Athens** - 21 Agias Theklas St, Athens: This modern hostel in the trendy Psirri neighborhood of Athens offers private rooms and dorms, a rooftop bar, and a game room.

- **Paraga Beach Hostel** - Paraga Beach, Mykonos: This beachfront hostel in Mykonos offers private rooms and dorms, a swimming pool, and a beach bar.

- **Hostel Bay** - Agios Nikolaos, Crete: This modern hostel in Agios Nikolaos offers private rooms and dorms, a rooftop terrace, and a bar.

- **Bedbox Hostel** - 8 Kapodistriou St, Thessaloniki: This hip hostel in Thessaloniki offers private rooms and dorms, a rooftop terrace, and a bar.

- **Faros I Hostel -** 31 Akti Miaouli, Piraeus: This waterfront hostel in Piraeus offers private rooms and dorms, a terrace with views of the harbor, and a bar.

- **The Island -** Agia Anna Beach, Naxos: This beachfront hostel in Naxos offers private rooms and dorms, a swimming pool, and a beach bar.

- **Hostel Plakias -** Plakias, Crete: This laid-back hostel in Plakias offers private rooms and dorms, a terrace with sea views, and a bar.

- **Ballos Beach Hostel -** Falassarna Beach, Crete: This beachfront hostel in Falassarna Beach offers private rooms and dorms, a beach bar, and a terrace with views of the Aegean Sea.

Guesthouses

A distinctive and endearing method to experience Greek hospitality and culture is via guesthouses, often known as pensions. They provide straightforward, often rustic lodging options ranging from renovated farmhouses to conventional homes and cottages. A lot of guesthouses are run and managed by families, and they provide a friendly environment that makes visitors feel at home. They provide a more genuine experience of Greece since they are often found in more sleepy towns and villages, away from the crowded tourist regions.

In Greece, traditional furniture and regional art are often used to adorn guesthouses. They could provide several room varieties, such as single, double, and family rooms, as well as inexpensive hostel-style lodging. While some provide private restrooms, public bathrooms are common in guesthouses. Moreover, they could feature common facilities for eating, relaxing, and gatherings, such as terraces, gardens, and outside patios.

The chance to sample local food and culture is one of the key benefits of staying at guesthouses. Fresh fish, grilled meats, and regional veggies are common elements in the home-cooked meals served by many guesthouses. Along with tasting local wine and spirits, visitors may also discover the region's traditions and customs.

The chance to meet locals and discover their way of life is another benefit of staying at guesthouses. Visitors may inquire about local attractions and activities, and they can even be asked to take part in festivals and other events. Compared to bigger hotels, guesthouses can provide a more individualized and private experience and may also include guided tours and other activities.

These are a few of Greece's top lodgings that provide guests with distinctive and genuine experiences:

To Perasma - Located in the historic village of Stemnitsa in the Peloponnese, To Perasma is a family-owned guesthouse that offers traditional accommodations and homemade meals. The guesthouse is housed in a 19th-century building that has been carefully restored to retain its original character.

Archontiko Anyfanti - Situated in the mountain village of Ano Pedina in the Zagori region of Epirus, Archontiko Anyfanti is a beautifully restored 18th-century mansion that offers luxurious guest rooms and suites. The guesthouse features traditional architecture and décor, with stone walls, wooden ceilings, and antique furnishings.

Vrahos Boutique Hotel - Located in the coastal town of Nafplio in the Peloponnese, Vrahos Boutique Hotel is a historic mansion that has been converted into a guesthouse. The guesthouse offers spacious and elegantly decorated rooms and suites, with views of the sea and the town's castle.

Theofilos Paradise - Situated in the village of Kastraki, near the Meteora monasteries in central Greece, Theofilos Paradise is a family-owned guesthouse that offers simple and comfortable accommodations in a scenic location. The guesthouse features a garden with views of the rock formations and serves homemade breakfast and dinner.

To Archontiko tis Anastasias - Located in the village of Ano Poroia in the Serres region of Macedonia, To Archontiko tis Anastasias is a traditional guesthouse that offers cozy and charming accommodations. The guesthouse features a garden with a fountain and a terrace with views of the surrounding hills.

Archontiko Dilofo - Situated in the village of Dilofo in the Zagori region of Epirus, Archontiko Dilofo is a historic mansion that has been converted into a guesthouse. The guesthouse offers comfortable and tastefully decorated rooms, as well as a garden with views of the mountains.

Unique Accommodation Options in Greece

In addition to traditional hotels, villas, apartments, and hostels, Greece also offers a variety of unique and unconventional accommodation options for travelers. These options offer a chance to experience Greece in a more unique and memorable way and range from luxury treehouses to cozy yurts.

Kapsaliana Village Hotel (Rethymno, Crete): Visitors have the opportunity to stay in original stone buildings that have been transformed into chic and contemporary hotel rooms in this beautifully renovated 17th-century town. The community has a restaurant, spa, and pool and is situated in a scenic area surrounded by olive orchards.

At Amaliada, Peloponnese, the Dexamenes Beach Hotel is housed in a former wine factory that has been transformed into opulent apartments. Large wine tanks and other vintage manufacturing elements have been preserved in the hotel, which also provides luxurious facilities and stunning ocean views.

The eco-friendly hotel Arcadia Blu in Nafplio, Peloponnese, allows visitors to stay in chic, cozy tents situated in a gorgeous olive grove. The hotel has a common kitchen and lounge space, and the tents are furnished with private bathrooms, air conditioning, and nice beds.

Mykonos Glamping (Mykonos, Cyclades): This opulent campground allows visitors to spend the night in chic tents situated in a tranquil setting with lovely sea views. The hotel has a restaurant, pool, and shuttle service to the beach, and the tents come with cozy mattresses, air conditioning, and private toilets.

The luxurious resort of Costa Navarino (Messenia, Peloponnese) has a range of distinctive lodging choices, including villas, suites, and rooms housed in old-fashioned stone towers. The resort has a spa, golf course, a number of restaurants, and bars in addition to its picturesque setting with lovely views of the ocean.

The River House is a renovated 18th-century stone home located on the banks of the Pineios River in Kalambaka, Thessaly. The home has been transformed into chic and comfortable guest rooms, and it also has a lovely garden, community kitchen, and living room.

Enastron Ecotourism is an eco-friendly hostel located in a magnificent setting surrounded by mountains and woods in Zagori, Epirus. The inn provides a range of lodging choices, including rooms and suites housed in old-world stone buildings. It also has a restaurant and outdoor activities.

Methana Volcano Resort (Methana, Peloponnese): This extraordinary resort is located on the crater of an extinct volcano and gives visitors the possibility to stay in chic, contemporary rooms and suites. The resort also has a restaurant, spa, and stunning ocean views.

Tholos Resort (Imerovigli, Santorini): This opulent resort provides visitors the possibility to stay in chic and cozy cave dwellings while it is situated in a scenic setting on the edge of a cliff. The homes are built into the cliff face and give stunning views of the sea, and the resort also features a pool, spa, and restaurant.

Historic stone homes in a lovely setting surrounded by olive orchards are available for tourists to stay in at the Arolithos Traditional Cretan Village in Heraklion, Crete. This traditional hamlet has been turned into a hotel. The community also has a restaurant, a swimming pool, and customary activities like cooking workshops and dance instruction.

In conclusion, Greece provides visitors with a wide range of unusual and unorthodox lodging choices, ranging from opulent treehouses to typical stone homes.

Chapter 16: Eating Out in Greece

Greek Cuisine: A Culinary Journey

Greek food is a real representation of the nation's many cultural influences and long history. Greece's food has been influenced by many different nations and customs, from the ancient Greeks to the Ottomans, creating a varied and delectable gastronomic experience.

The Mediterranean diet, which places an emphasis on using fresh, seasonal, and local foods, is at the core of Greek cuisine. The use of herbs, spices, and olive oil, which give dishes depth and complexity, is a hallmark of the cuisine. Greeks are renowned for their enjoyment of communal eating, making meals with family and friends a social event.

The Greek salad, which is created with tomatoes, cucumbers, feta cheese, red onion, and olives and flavored with oregano and olive oil, is one of the most well-known Greek foods. Other well-liked mezes (small meals) include dolmades, stuffed grape leaves filled with grains, herbs, and sometimes meat, and tzatziki, a yogurt, garlic, and cucumber dish.

Greek diet is heavy on seafood, and coastal areas provide a wide range of fresh fish and shellfish. Popular dishes include grilled octopus, fried calamari, and grilled sardines. Lamb and pork are the most popular meats used in meals, which are also frequent. A popular street snack is souvlaki, a skewered beef dish often accompanied by pita bread and tzatziki.

Moussaka, a layered casserole cooked with eggplant, ground beef, or lamb, and a rich béchamel sauce, is one of the most well-known Greek foods. Another well-liked meal is called pastitsio, which uses pasta in place of the eggplant. These meals are warming and hearty, ideal for a chilly evening.

The phyllo-based pastry known as spanakopita, which is stuffed with feta cheese and spinach, is another traditional Greek dish. Another favorite is tyropita, a similar pastry packed with cheese. The most famous kind of Greek cheese is feta, which is a feature of the cuisine. Graviera and kefalotyri are two more wonderful cheeses that are often used in cooking.

Greek cuisine has a strong emphasis on desserts, offering a wide range of sweet delights. Among the most well-known is baklava, a pastry comprised of layers of phyllo dough, honey, and almonds. Other sweets include loukoumades, fried doughnuts drenched in honey syrup, and galaktoboureko, a pastry filled with custard.

Each area of Greece has its own distinct cuisine and specialties in addition to these traditional foods. For instance, the island of Crete is well-known for its native cheese, graviera, as well as its use of regional herbs and spices like oregano and thyme. Cherry tomatoes, which are used in several cuisines, including the well-known tomato fritters, are renowned for being grown on the Greek island of Santorini.

Greek wine also merits consideration; it has a distinguished past that dates back to antiquity. Several indigenous grape types are grown throughout the nation, including the white Assyrtiko and the red Agiorgitiko, which provide distinctive and tasty wines. A traditional

Greek wine that is recommended is called retsina and is flavored with pine resin.

The dining experience in Greece is one of the culinary highlights in addition to the mouthwatering food and wine. In addition to savoring the cuisine and the companionship of their loved ones, Greeks take their time during meals. Tavernas (traditional Greek eateries) are fantastic places to have a meal and experience the local culture since they often feature a laid-back and hospitable ambiance.

Greek food is a varied and fascinating gastronomic trip that reflects the historical and cultural influences of the nation.

Regional Greek Foods to Try

Greek cuisine is known for its fresh, wholesome ingredients and flavorful dishes. But beyond the classic dishes like moussaka and souvlaki, each region of Greece has its own unique culinary traditions and specialties. Here are some regional Greek foods to try on your next trip to Greece:

Santorini Fava - This is a type of yellow split pea that is grown on the island of Santorini. It is often made into a puree with olive oil, onions, and lemon juice and served as a dip or spread.

Kefalonian Meat Pie - This dish is a specialty of the island of Kefalonia and consists of a phyllo pastry filled with ground beef, onion, and potatoes. It is typically served as a main course and is a hearty and flavorful dish.

Mykonian Spicy Cheese - This cheese is made on the island of Mykonos and is typically served as a spread with bread. It is made with local goat's milk and has a spicy kick from the addition of chili flakes.

Cretan Dakos - This is a simple but delicious dish from the island of Crete. It consists of a barley rusk topped with chopped tomatoes, feta cheese, and olive oil. It is a refreshing and light snack or appetizer.

Thessaloniki Bougatsa - This is a pastry that originated in the city of Thessaloniki and is made with phyllo pastry, semolina custard, and a dusting of powdered sugar. It is a popular breakfast pastry and can be found at bakeries throughout the city.

Ioannina Perama Cheese - This cheese is made in the town of Ioannina and is a semi-hard cheese made from sheep's milk. It has a distinct, slightly smoky flavor and is often served as a table cheese or grated over pasta dishes.

Sifnos Revithada - This is a traditional chickpea stew that is a specialty of the island of Sifnos. It is made with chickpeas, onions, garlic, and olive oil and is typically slow-cooked in a clay pot for several hours.

Messinian Kalamata Olives - These olives are grown in the region of Messinia and are known for their deep, rich flavor. They are often served as a snack or added to salads and other dishes for a burst of flavor.

Mani Pork Sausage - This sausage is made in the Mani region of the Peloponnese and is seasoned with garlic, oregano, and other herbs. It is often grilled or pan-fried and is a popular dish in the region.

Ikarian Soufiko - This is a vegetable stew that originated on the island of Ikaria. It is made with a variety of vegetables, including eggplant, zucchini, and tomatoes, and is often flavored with herbs like oregano and thyme.

These are just a few of the many regional Greek foods to try on your next trip to Greece. Whether you're a foodie looking to explore the unique culinary traditions of each region or simply looking to try new and delicious dishes, Greek cuisine has something to offer for everyone.

Greek Wine: An Overview

Greece is regarded as one of the oldest wine-producing areas in the world, having produced wine for thousands of years. Greece is renowned for its distinctive grape varieties, varied geography, and conventional wine-making methods. Greece's wines are becoming more well-known in recent years, although not having the same reputation as some other nations for wine.

More than 300 native grape varietals, many of which are unique to Greece, may be found there. Greek consumers like the grape varieties Agiorgitiko, Assyrtiko, Malagousia, Moschofilero, and Xinomavro among others. These grape varieties may be used to make a variety of wines, from light and crisp whites to robust and complex reds.

Greece's terroir is similarly varied, with several microclimates and soil types found across the nation. For instance, the volcanic soils of the Aegean islands are well-known, but the soils of the Peloponnese are rich in limestone. The distinctive characteristics of Greek wines are a result of these distinctive terroirs.

Greek wine is likewise created utilizing time-honored methods that have been handed down through the centuries. Several wineries still use techniques like foot-stomping grapes and maturing wines in amphorae, which are clay jars. Greek wine's distinctive personality is preserved thanks to these age-old methods.

The island of Santorini in the Aegean Sea is one of the most well-known wine-producing areas in Greece. The Assyrtiko grape variety and the volcanic soils of Santorini are renowned for producing crisp, mineral-forward white wines. Some of the most distinctive and premium white wines in the world are produced on the island because of its peculiar terroir and wine-making methods.

The Peloponnese, which is the birthplace of the Agiorgitiko grape variety, is another well-known wine area in Greece. With aromas of black fruit, spice, and earthy undertones, this grape creates robust and intricate red wines. Mavrodaphne, a sweet red wine produced in the area from the Mavrodaphne grape variety, is also well-known. It tastes of caramel, chocolate, and dried fruit.

Other important wine-producing areas in Greece include Crete, which is recognized for its red wines produced from the Kotsifali and Mandilaria grape varieties, and Macedonia, which is famous for its Xinomavro grape variety.

Greek wine pairs well with Mediterranean food because of its rich flavors and sharp acidity, which go particularly well with grilled fish, lamb, and fresh vegetables. Greek wine is often paired with popular foods like spanakopita, moussaka, and tzatziki.

With a variety of grape varieties, terroirs, and conventional wine-making methods, Greek wine delivers a distinct and one-of-a-kind personality. Greek wine is definitely worth discovering, regardless of your level of wine experience or your level of interest.

Greece is renowned today for producing a broad range of wines, from crisp and light whites to robust reds. Greek wine varieties including Assyrtiko, Agiorgitiko, Xinomavro, and Moschofilero are some of the most well-liked worldwide.

The white wine variety known as Assyrtiko is mostly cultivated on the island of Santorini. It is often likened to French wines from the Loire Valley because of its sharp acidity and minerality. Seafood, salads, and other light foods go nicely with Assyrtiko, a versatile wine.

A red wine variety called Agiorgitiko is mostly cultivated in the Nemea area of the Peloponnese. The wine has a substantial body, juicy fruit aromas, and a peppery finish. Grilled meats, stews, and other substantial foods go nicely with agorgitiko.

Red wine variety Xinomavro is mostly cultivated in Macedonia's Northern Greece area. It is a full-bodied, rich wine with strong tannins and flavors of earth, spice, and black cherry. Strong cheeses, stews, and roasted meats go nicely with Xinomavro.

White wine grape Moschofilero is mostly cultivated in the Peloponnese. With flowery and citrus aromas and fresh acidity, it is a light and energizing wine. Salads, light seafood meals, and other light foods go nicely with mochofilero.

Greece is renowned for making a range of dessert wines, including Vinsanto and Mavrodaphne, in addition to these well-liked varieties.

Vinsanto is a sweet wine that is mostly manufactured on the island of Santorini from sun-dried grapes. Mavrodaphne is a sweet fortified wine that is mostly manufactured in the Peloponnese from the grape variety of the same name.

Greece is home to several wineries, many of which are situated in scenic and ancient regions. Santorini, Nemea, and Naoussa are a few of Greece's most well-known wine-producing areas.

Greek wine has recently become more well-known and respected on a global scale, with many wine experts and connoisseurs applauding the variety and high quality of Greek wines. As a consequence, a lot of Greek vineyards have started exporting their wines to other nations.

Greek culture and food are rich and energetic, much like Greek wine. There is a Greek wine that is likely to fit your interests and preferences, whether you are a wine aficionado or just enjoy a glass of wine with a satisfying meal.

Best Places to Eat in Athens, the Greek Islands, and Beyond

When it comes to Greek cuisine, there are endless options for delicious dining. From the bustling streets of Athens to the tranquil beaches of the Greek islands, travelers can find amazing food and drink throughout the country. Here are some of the best places to eat in Athens, the Greek islands, and beyond:

Athens:

Klimataria - This historic taverna in the neighborhood of Plaka has been serving traditional Greek cuisine for over 90 years. Try the moussaka or the grilled lamb chops.

Address: Plaka, 7 Agias Theklas Street, Athens 10554, Greece

Ta Karamanlidika Tou Fani - A deli and restaurant specializing in cured meats, cheeses, and traditional meze dishes. Try the smoked pork loin and the feta with honey and sesame.

Address: Agiou Fanouriou 1, Athens 105 53, Greece

Spondi - A Michelin-starred restaurant in the Pangrati neighborhood, known for its creative Greek and French fusion cuisine. Try the lobster with orzo and the sea bass with artichokes.

Address: Pyrronos 5, Athina 116 36, Greece

Greek Islands:

Avli Tou Thodori - A beachside taverna on the island of Santorini, known for its fresh seafood and Mediterranean cuisine. Try the grilled octopus and the fried tomato balls.

Address: Beach of Perivolos, Santorini 847 03, Greece

Taverna Nikolas - A family-run taverna on the island of Naxos, known for its traditional Greek dishes and friendly atmosphere. Try the stuffed bell peppers and the beef stifado.

Address: Agios Prokopios, Naxos 843 00, Greece

Melenio Cafe - A cozy cafe and bakery on the island of Corfu, known for its homemade sweets and pastries. Try the baklava and the galaktoboureko.

Address: 15 Theotoki St., Corfu 491 00, Greece

Other Regions:

To Kanoni - A seafood restaurant in the town of Preveza, known for its fresh fish and traditional Greek dishes. Try the grilled sardines and the seafood risotto.

Address: Kanoni, Preveza 481 00, Greece

Agora - A restaurant in the city of Thessaloniki, known for its modern Greek cuisine and innovative cocktails. Try the pork belly with orange and the olive oil cake.

Address: Athonos 33, Thessaloniki 546 23, Greece

Tsipouradiko Karamanlidika - A tsipouro bar and meze restaurant in the city of Athens, known for its selection of cured meats and cheeses. Try the sausage and cheese platter and the fried feta balls.

Address: Sokratous 1, Athens 105 52, Greece

Greece has a rich culinary history, and these restaurants offer just a small taste of the amazing food and drink that can be found throughout the country. Whether you're looking for traditional Greek dishes or modern fusion cuisine, there is something for everyone in Greece.

Part VII: Travel Essentials

Chapter 17: Money Matters and Communication

Currency and Exchange Rates

While going abroad, even to Greece, it's crucial to take currency and exchange rates into account. The official currency of Greece is the euro, which is also the currency of many other European nations. Almost 340 million people use the euro, which is used by 19 nations in the Eurozone and is the second most traded currency in the world behind the US dollar.

The value of the euro swings in relation to a number of other currencies, including the US dollar, the British pound, and the Japanese yen. Travel expenses and the cost of goods and services in the local currency are both impacted by exchange rates. While visiting Greece, it's critical to comprehend how currency rates operate and how to get the most for your money.

In the foreign currency market, supply and demand dictate exchange rates. Many variables, including current political and economic developments, central bank policies, and market mood, have an impact on this market. The cost of travel and the value of assets may be affected by changes in a currency's exchange rate over time.

It's crucial to understand the current exchange rate between the euro and your own currency before visiting Greece. This might assist you in estimating the cost of your vacation, choosing how much cash to carry, and planning your spending. In Greece, there are several places to convert currencies, including banks, exchange offices, and airports. When converting money, it's vital to evaluate exchange rates and fees since they might differ.

Using a credit card with no international transaction fees is one approach to obtaining the best currency rate while visiting Greece. By doing this, you may save money and receive the best possible conversion rate for your purchases. Moreover, it is a good idea to let your bank or credit card provider know about your vacation intentions as they could stop transactions that seem strange or suspicious.

In Greece, ATMs are widely dispersed and provide a quick means to get local cash. However certain ATMs could tack on extra charges, so it's crucial to check with your bank to determine if there are any limitations or costs associated with using international ATMs. Keep an eye on your account balance and make sure you have enough money on hand to pay your bills.

Currency and exchange rates are significant elements to take into account while visiting Greece. You can plan your costs and make the most of your vacation by knowing how currency rates operate and how to obtain the greatest value for your money. It's crucial to examine rates and fees to make sure you're receiving the best deal whether you decide to use a credit card, an ATM, or a bank to convert money.

Using Credit Cards and ATMs in Greece

Greece is a modern country with a well-developed banking system, and credit cards and ATMs are widely accepted throughout the country. However, it is still a good idea to be prepared with cash, particularly in smaller towns and villages, where cash is often the preferred method of payment.

Credit Cards:

Major credit cards such as Visa, Mastercard, and American Express are accepted at most hotels, restaurants, and shops in Greece, particularly in popular tourist destinations. It is always a good idea to inform your bank of your travel plans before departing to ensure that your card is not blocked due to suspicious activity.

In some cases, particularly at smaller establishments, there may be a minimum amount required for credit card transactions or a surcharge for using a card. It is always a good idea to check with the establishment before making a purchase.

ATMs:

Greece has a considerable number of ATMs, especially in the major towns and popular tourist areas. Major foreign debit and credit cards are often accepted at ATMs, and the exchange rate is typically favorable. It is crucial to inquire with your bank about any possible costs associated with overseas transactions or currency conversion.

It may be necessary to make repeated withdrawals from different ATMs in order to get the required quantity of cash since certain

ATMs have a restriction on the amount that can be withdrawn in a single transaction.

To reduce the danger of theft, it is always a good idea to utilize ATMs that are housed in banks or in well-lit places. Always cover the keypad while entering your PIN and be mindful of gadgets that might be used to steal card information, such as skimming devices.

Currency Exchange:

While it is possible to convert money in banks, exchange offices, and some hotels, taking cash out of an ATM is often more practical. When converting money, it's critical to understand the exchange rate and any potential costs since they might differ significantly.

In general, it is not advised to convert money at airports or other popular tourist destinations since the exchange rates and costs could be higher.

In Greece, credit cards and ATMs are extensively used, making it simple for visitors to acquire money and make transactions. But it's still a good idea to have cash on hand, especially in smaller towns and villages where it's often the preferred means of payment. Be mindful of any costs that could apply to currency conversion or overseas transactions, and use care at all times while using ATMs to reduce your risk of identity theft.

Buying a SIM Card in Greece

It's important to maintain contact with your loved ones and the internet when traveling to Greece. Purchasing a local SIM card is one of the simplest and most cheap methods to remain connected. The finest providers, how to get a SIM card in Greece, and important information regarding pricing and plans will all be covered in this post.

Ensure that your phone is unlocked before beginning the process of purchasing a SIM card in Greece. Your phone could be tied to that carrier's network if you bought it from them. You may utilize a third-party service to unlock your phone or contact your carrier to get one.

You may buy a SIM card from a number of service providers, such as Cosmote, Vodafone, and Wind after your phone has been unlocked. Prepaid and postpaid plans with a range of data allocations and features are available from these providers.

In most towns and popular tourist destinations, you may find a mobile phone shop or kiosk where you can buy a SIM card. You must provide your passport or other forms of identification together with your Greek address. The procedure is simple and generally just only a few minutes.

Depending on the company and plan you choose, a SIM card in Greece might cost anywhere from €10 to €60. Prepaid plans often cost less money and provide greater flexibility. A SIM card typically costs between 10 and 20 euros, and it often comes with some initial credit for calls and data.

After buying a SIM card, you must activate it by contacting customer care at the provider's number or going to their website. To activate your plan, you may also need to deposit credit to your account. The majority of service providers give top-up alternatives through their website, mobile app, or physical location.

You may use your phone for calls, text messaging, and data after your SIM card has been activated. You may use your phone as you normally would at home, but if you are not on an unlimited plan, data use can soon pile up. To make sure that your phone is linked to the proper network, you may also need to change the APN settings on it.

You may utilize your phone's roaming features in addition to buying a local SIM card to remain connected when visiting Greece. Unfortunately, roaming fees may be high, and coverage and internet speed difficulties could arise. It's usually a good idea to check with your carrier about their foreign roaming charges and rules before you depart.

The most convenient and economical method to remain connected while traveling is to get a SIM card in Greece. You may reap the rewards of keeping connected on your journey by doing some research to identify the best provider and prepare for your requirements.

Chapter 18: Transportation Apps and Resources in Greece

Useful Apps for Getting Around in Greece

It might be difficult to navigate Greece as a tourist, particularly if this is your first trip there. Thankfully, a variety of mobile apps have been created to aid travelers in easily navigating the nation thanks to the advancement of technology. These applications provide details on accommodations, local activities, transportation, and other helpful travel-related information. We'll look at some of the best navigational apps for Greece in this post.

OASA Telematics

The official app for the Athens public transportation system is called OASA Telematics. You may easily plan your route with the real-time information on bus, subway, and tram timetables that is provided. The app also has a route planner that suggests the optimal path to travel depending on where you are now and where you want to go. In order to help you plan your route, the app also gives information on the expected time of arrival for each vehicle.

Beat

In Athens, Thessaloniki, and other Greek cities, Beat is a ride-hailing service. With only a few touches on your smartphone, you may call a taxi or a private vehicle. Beat offers transparent pricing so that you are aware of your costs before you set off on your adventure. The app also has a rating system that enables you to give your driver comments and score your overall experience.

BlaBlaCar

A car-sharing app called BlaBlaCar is available in Greece and other nations all over the globe. You may split the cost of a ride with other passengers, which can lower your carbon impact and enable you to save money. The app offers details about the driver, the car, and the trip's cost. It also has a rating system that enables you to comment on your experience and evaluate the driver.

Visit Greece

The official app of the Greek National Tourism Authority is called Visit Greece. It helps you arrange your schedule by providing information about nearby events, sights, and activities. The app has a map that you can use to find lodgings, dining options, and activities in the area. It also offers useful information, such as emergency numbers and weather predictions.

XE Currency

XE Currency is a currency converter app that provides real-time exchange rates for over 180 currencies. It allows you to convert currency on the go, helping you avoid any misunderstandings or overcharges. The app also includes a calculator, which allows you to make quick and easy calculations based on the latest exchange rates.

Google Maps

A mapping and navigation program called Google Maps offers directions, traffic updates, and details on nearby businesses. Since it offers precise information on public transportation, driving instructions, and walking routes, it is crucial software for navigating Greece. The app also provides details on nearby eateries, lodging options, and attractions.

Airbnb

With the help of the well-known lodging search engine Airbnb, you may locate inexpensive accommodations in Greece that are also distinctive. It offers a variety of lodging choices, ranging from individual rooms to full complexes and villas. You may also use the app to read reviews and ratings left by prior visitors before making a reservation for lodging.

For visitors to Greece, these applications might be of great use. They provide helpful information on lodging, local activities, transit, and other travel-related topics, assisting you in making vacation plans and navigating the nation with ease. With the aid of these applications, you can maximize your stay in Greece and take advantage of all that this stunning nation has to offer.

Booking Transportation and Tours in Greece

To make the most of your time and experience everything that Greece has to offer, it's crucial to take transportation and excursions into account when making travel plans. Thankfully, there are many possibilities in Greece for reserving travel and excursions, both in advance and right away. Here are some suggestions and choices for scheduling travel and activities in Greece:

Flights: In order to receive the cheapest prices, it's crucial to book your flights in advance if you're traveling to Greece. Aegean Airlines, Olympic Air, and Ryanair are just a few of the airlines that fly to Greece. The airline's website or a third-party website like Expedia or Kayak are both options for booking flights.

Ferries: You'll probably need to board a ferry if you want to explore the Greek islands. Greece is home to various ferry operators, such as Blue Star Ferries, Hellenic Seaways, and Anek Lines. On the ferry company's website or a third-party website like Ferryhopper or Direct Ferries, you may purchase ferry tickets in advance.

Trains: Greece does not have any high-speed trains, although there are a number of regional trains that travel around the nation. At the railway station or online via the Hellenic Railways website, passengers may buy train tickets.

Buses: In Greece, buses are a typical means of transportation. Many bus companies provide services all across the nation. Bus tickets may be purchased at the bus station or online at the KTEL website.

Car rentals: Renting a vehicle might be a wonderful alternative if you wish to explore Greece alone. Greece is home to a number of automobile rental businesses, including Avis, Europcar, and Hertz. Either at the airport upon arrival or in advance online, you may hire a vehicle.

Guided tours: Greece has a number of tour providers, including Viator, GetYourGuide, and Athens Walking Tours, if you wish to go on a guided tour. Tours may be booked online ahead of time or when you get there at the tour operator's office.

Private tours: You may book a private tour with a local guide if you're seeking a more individualized experience. Private tours are provided by a number of businesses in Greece, including Withlocals, Greeking.me, and Keytours. Online reservations for private tours are available.

It's crucial to read reviews and do thorough research before making reservations for transportation and tours in Greece to be sure you're receiving a trustworthy provider with excellent service. During the busiest travel times, it's also a good idea to make reservations in advance since popular routes and trips tend to sell out rapidly. To make the most of your vacation, you may simply reserve transportation and excursions in Greece with a little preparation and study.

Helpful Websites for Planning Your Trip to Greece

When planning a trip to Greece, there are many helpful websites available that can provide a wealth of information on everything from accommodation to transportation to sightseeing. Here are some of the most useful websites for planning your trip to Greece:

Visit Greece (www.visitgreece.gr): This is the official tourism website of Greece, providing a wealth of information on everything from culture and history to beaches and cuisine. The website offers extensive guides on various destinations throughout the country, including Athens, the Greek islands, and lesser-known regions of Greece. Visitors can also find information on events and festivals, transportation, and practical information for travelers.

Athens Info Guide (www.athensinfoguide.com): This website offers a comprehensive guide to Athens, providing information on everything from sightseeing and nightlife to accommodation and transportation. The site includes detailed guides on popular tourist attractions in Athens, such as the Acropolis, the National Archaeological Museum, and the Plaka neighborhood. Visitors can also find practical information on public transportation, taxi services, and other essential services.

Greeka (www.greeka.com): Greeka is a popular travel website that offers a wide range of information on Greece, including guides on popular destinations and attractions, hotels, tours, and activities. The site is particularly useful for those planning a trip to the Greek islands, with detailed guides on popular islands such as Santorini, Mykonos, and Crete.

Ferry Hopper (www.ferryhopper.com): If you plan on visiting the Greek islands, Ferry Hopper is an essential tool for planning your ferry travel. The website allows you to search and book ferry tickets for all major ferry routes in Greece, including those between the islands and the mainland. Ferry Hopper also offers useful information on ferry schedules, prices, and travel times.

Greek Travel Pages (www.gtp.gr): Greek Travel Pages is a comprehensive directory of travel-related businesses in Greece, including hotels, car rental agencies, tour operators, and more. The website offers a search function that allows visitors to easily find businesses in specific locations or categories. Greek Travel Pages also provides news and information on travel-related topics in Greece.

Discover Greek Culture (www.discovergreekculture.com): This website offers a unique perspective on Greek culture and history, with detailed guides on ancient sites, museums, and other cultural attractions. The site also includes articles on Greek food, wine, and other aspects of Greek culture. Visitors can book tours and activities through the website, and also find practical information on transportation and other essential services.

Lonely Planet Greece (www.lonelyplanet.com/greece): The Greece section of Lonely Planet's website is an excellent resource for independent travelers, offering detailed guides on popular destinations throughout Greece. The site includes information on attractions, accommodations, transportation, and other practical information for travelers. Visitors can also purchase guidebooks and maps through the website.

TripAdvisor (www.tripadvisor.com): TripAdvisor is a popular travel website that offers reviews and ratings of hotels, restaurants, and attractions throughout Greece. Visitors can use the site to research accommodations and activities and to read reviews from other travelers. TripAdvisor also provides a search function that allows visitors to find businesses in specific locations or categories.

These are just a few of the many helpful websites available for planning your trip to Greece. By taking advantage of these resources, you can make the most of your time in this beautiful and historic country.

Useful Greek Words and Phrases

Knowing a few useful words and phrases in the local language can be very helpful when traveling to a foreign country. Greece is no exception, and while many Greeks speak English, especially in tourist areas, it is always appreciated when visitors make an effort to speak Greek.

Here are some useful Greek words and phrases to know when visiting Greece:

- Γεια σου (Yia sou) - Hello (informal)
- Γεια σας (Yia sas) - Hello (formal)
- Καλημέρα (Kalimera) - Good morning
- Καλησπέρα (Kalispera) - Good evening
- Καληνύχτα (Kalinichta) - Good night
- Συγνώμη (Signomi) - Excuse me/Sorry
- Ευχαριστώ (Efharisto) - Thank you
- Παρακαλώ (Parakalo) - Please
- Ναι (Ne) - Yes
- Όχι (Ohi) - No
- Πόσο κοστίζει αυτό; (Poso kostizi afto?) - How much does this cost?
- Πού είναι η τουαλέτα; (Pu ine i tualeta?) - Where is the bathroom/toilet?
- Μιλάτε αγγλικά; (Milate anglika?) - Do you speak English?
- Πώς πάω στο...; (Pos pao sto...?) - How do I get to...?

These are just a few basic words and phrases to get started, but there are many more to learn. It can also be helpful to learn some food and drink vocabulary, such as:

- Καφές (Kafes) - Coffee

- Νερό (Nero) - Water
- Μπύρα (Bira) - Beer
- Κρασί (Krasi) - Wine
- Τυρί (Tiri) - Cheese
- Ψωμί (Psomi) - Bread
- Μεζέδες (Mezedes) - Small plates/tapas
- Σαλάτα (Salata) - Salad
- Κεφτέδες (Keftedes) - Meatballs
- Μουσακάς (Mousakas) - A traditional Greek dish with eggplant, minced meat, and béchamel sauce

In addition to learning some basic words and phrases, it can be helpful to download language apps or phrasebooks to your phone or carry a small phrasebook with you. This can help you communicate better with locals and make your trip more enjoyable.

CONCLUSION

In conclusion, Greece is a nation that is abundant in natural beauty, cultural diversity, and historical significance. This beautiful location offers a diverse range of attractions, from the historic sites of Athens to the picture-perfect shores of the Greek islands, so there is something for everyone to enjoy here.

During the course of this book, we have investigated various aspects of Greece, such as its history and mythology, as well as its art, architecture, and food, among other topics. We have covered a lot of ground when it comes to the specifics of trip preparation for Greece, such as the many modes of transportation, the accommodations available, and the useful websites and applications. In addition, we have spoken about responsible and sustainable tourist practices, with an emphasis on the need of preserving Greece's natural and cultural treasures for the benefit of future generations.

One of the things that makes Greece so remarkable is its varied and mouthwatering food, which is characterized by its use of fresh ingredients and one-of-a-kind regional delicacies. We sampled a wide variety of meals and wines from Greece, including well-known dishes like moussaka and souvlaki as well as lesser-known regional specialties like kleftiko and kokoretsi.

Ohi Day and the Athens Marathon are just two of the numerous unique festivals and events that take place throughout the year in Greece. Participating in these events gives attendees a one-of-a-kind chance to directly engage with aspects of Greek culture and heritage.

Last but not least, we have included an overview of some of the most popular travel spots in Greece, such as the city of Athens, the Greek islands, and the Mani Peninsula. Each of these areas has something unique to offer, from the well-known attractions of Athens to the picture-perfect beaches of the islands to the breathtaking natural scenery of the Mani.

In general, Greece is a destination that caters to tourists of all ages and is filled with activities that cater to a wide variety of interests. Greece is likely to fulfill your expectations, no matter what you're looking for: rich history and culture, breathtaking natural scenery, or mouthwatering cuisine and wine. We hope that at the end of this book, you will have not only the knowledge but also the inspiration you need to organize a journey to Greece that will live long in the memory.

REFERENCES

Chrissy. (2022, April 17). A Local's Guide to Public Transport in Greece - Greece Travel Ideas. Retrieved February 16, 2023, from Greece Travel Ideas website: https://greecetravelideas.com/public-transport-in-greece/

Made in United States
Orlando, FL
31 March 2023

31555301R00196